Hearing the Other Side

Deliberative versus Participatory Democracy

"Religion and politics," as the old saying goes, "should never be discussed in mixed company." And yet fostering discussions that cross lines of political difference has long been a central concern of political theorists. More recently, it has also become a cause célèbre for pundits and civic-minded citizens wanting to improve the health of American democracy. But only recently have scholars begun empirical investigations of where and with what consequences people interact with those whose political views differ from their own. *Hearing the Other Side* examines this theme in the context of the contemporary United States. It is unique in its effort to link political theory with empirical research. Drawing on her empirical work, Mutz concludes that it is doubtful that an extremely activist political culture can also be a heavily deliberative one.

Diana C. Mutz is Samuel A. Stouffer Professor of Political Science and Communication at the University of Pennsylvania, where she serves as Director of the Institute for the Study of Citizens and Politics at the Annenberg Public Policy Center. Mutz received her Ph.D. from Stanford University in 1988. She has published articles involving public opinion, political psychology, and political communication in a variety of academic journals, including the *American Political Science Review*, the *American Journal of Political Science, Public Opinion Quarterly, Journal of Politics*, and *Journal of Communication*. She is also the author of *Impersonal Influence: How Perceptions of Mass Collectives Affect Political Attitudes* (1998), which was awarded the 1999 Robert Lane Prize for the Best Book in Political Psychology by the American Political Science Association and the 2004 Doris Graber Prize for Most Influential Book on Political Communication published in the last ten years.

D0107453

Hearing the Other Side

Deliberative versus Participatory Democracy

DIANA C. MUTZ
University of Pennsylvania

CAMBRIDGE
UNIVERSITY PRESS

CAMBRIDGE UNIVERSITY PRESS
Cambridge, New York, Melbourne, Madrid, Cape Town, Singapore,
São Paulo, Delhi, Dubai, Tokyo, Mexico City

Cambridge University Press
The Edinburgh Building, Cambridge CB2 8RU, UK

Published in the United States of America by Cambridge University Press, New York

www.cambridge.org
Information on this title: www.cambridge.org/9780521612289

First published 2006

A catalogue record for this publication is available from the British Library

Library of Congress Cataloging in Publication Data
Mutz, Diana Carole
Hearing the other side : deliberative versus participatory democracy /
Diana C. Mutz.
p. cm.
Includes bibliographical references and index.
isbn 0-521-84750-8 (hardback) – isbn 0-521-61228-4 (pbk.)
1. Political sociology. 2. Social networks – Political aspects.
3. Communication – Political aspects. 4. Political culture. I. Title.
ja76.m88 2006
306.2–dc22   2005021891

ISBN 978-0-521-84750-6 Hardback
ISBN 978-0-521-61228-9 Paperback

For Walden, Maria, and Simone,
and that world I cannot visit, not even in my dreams

Contents

Preface

This is not the book I wanted to write. For this reason, among others, it has taken me much longer than I had anticipated to determine the real storyline. My hope is that my patience pays off, and in the end it rings truer to the world of real political experience as a result. It still does not, for better or worse, have the kind of neat and tidy ending that I originally sought. But in this case, that is probably as it should be because I believe the dilemma I describe has no easy solution. Nonetheless, it provides a distinct tension in American politics, one that remains largely neglected in both theory and empirical work.

After I gave up on my original book – a book evaluating the extent to which empirical evidence substantiates the claims of deliberative democratic theory – I remained bothered by the extent to which other scholars viewed my work on political networks as inconsistent, self-contradictory, and even schizophrenic. In particular, the empirical work featured in Chapters 3 and 4 of this book evoked this reaction. Technical details on these two studies can be found in articles published in the *American Political Science Review* and the *American Journal of Political Science*. Because these two pieces had seemingly contradictory things to say about the consequences of cross-cutting political networks for democratic well-being, many assumed that at least one of them (and maybe both) had gotten things wrong. In the end, these reactions were extremely valuable in that they prompted me to embark upon a broader consideration of the nature of social and political life and their frequent intersections.

In the process of writing this book, I have benefited from many wonderful colleagues at my home universities and elsewhere. These people include Andy Baker, Sigal Ben-Porath, Bob Huckfeldt, Kathleen Hall Jamieson, Shiloh Krieger, Jon Krosnick, Jocelyn Landau, Jeff Mondak, Tom Nelson, Paul Martin, Kathleen McGraw, and Paul Sniderman. The data collection for this project was originally funded by The Spencer Foundation as a study of how citizens' political educations are furthered by non–like-minded political company. The survey was fielded by the University of Wisconsin Survey Center under the direction of Bob Lee. Several years later, the Center for Advanced Study in the Behavioral Sciences gave me time to do the additional reading and writing that eventually turned these ideas into a book. The generosity of Leonore and Walter Annenberg provided me with an especially stimulating environment in which to continue studying important issues in political communication.

In many ways an additional group of people has contributed to this book, though they are, for the most part, completely unaware of its existence. These are the committed political activists who exemplify the very tension described in this book. Beyond what my academic colleagues have taught me, I learned a great deal about the political world from growing up in the midst of political activism. My earliest instruction in politics consisted of stuffing envelopes, using a staple gun to put up yard signs, struggling to remain awake during a Lincoln Day Dinner speech (the same one, for the nth time), going door to door canvassing for a candidate, and enduring endless paper cuts while sealing direct mail envelopes. There were some years when I attended literally dozens of county fairs, where I learned about the latest innovations in farm equipment, admired the award-winning steer, and talked shop with people who probably shared very little with me in terms of their everyday interests and concerns. I learned that practical politics involved a certain amount of reaching out to people, at least it did if you wanted to win. Some support would come from quarters that the campaigns themselves found quite baffling. But if you wanted to win, you didn't question the basis of your supporters' ardor.

These reminiscences from my childhood may seem quaint in an era of mass mediated politics, but versions of these same activities continue today. They may be dinners to raise money for television ad campaigns, or to pay professional direct mail companies, but they still involve activists, those who ardently support a political cause or candidate, and freely give of their time and money toward these ends.

For my lessons in real-world politics I thank Mike McDaniel (who knows why there was always a basketball in the bathroom), Dr. Fred Risk, D.D.S., and my father, John Mutz. These three know all too well the thrill of political activism, and the kind of grueling commitment involved in public life.

And finally, I thank my husband, Robin, for serving as my most constructive critic, and Walden, Maria, and Simi, for denying me the ivory tower academic life and insisting on a much fuller, more grounded existence. The many perspectives they give me on the political world as it sifts through everyday life are invaluable not only to my work, but especially to my happiness.

I

Hearing the Other Side, in Theory and in Practice

When I was a child my father and I often went to the dentist together because the office was downtown, near his office, and because it was *his* dentist, the one he had seen since childhood, and my dad wanted very badly for me to like him. I made it clear that I had mixed feelings about the guy. Even if I could get over his name (Dr. Risk), and the fact that he insisted on calling me "Missy," there was the fact that he was independently wealthy and practiced dentistry *for fun*.

But the ritual between the two of them was well established. He would put my father in the chair, stuff his mouth full of cotton, and begin to talk politics. As president of the local American Civil Liberties Union chapter, Dr. Risk and my ardently Republican father had a lot to talk about. My father could barely contain his eagerness to spit just to get a word in edgewise. For the two of them it was sport, and it was clear that my father greatly respected Dr. Risk, even if he would never take political advice from him. I know this because if I ever complained about going to the dentist, my father would nudge me with guilt: "But Dr. Risk is such a good man." Good man or not, he was, after all, a dentist.

My own political conversations with my father are not always so enjoyable. There is sometimes the uneasy feeling that perhaps the apple has fallen too far from the tree. Our conversations take the form of a delicate dance of approaching, backing off, and approaching again, that tension that is so characteristic of relationships involving love and affection as well as disagreement. In relationships of this kind, most of us understandably find it easier to talk about things other than politics, to seek safer ground.

And yet we are told by many that these are conversations we need to have. Not necessarily with our relatives perhaps, but in order to be good citizens and compassionate human beings, we are told we need to hear the other side, whether we like it or not. This observation was my point of departure for this book. I wanted to know where people came into contact with political ideas they disliked, how they handled the situation, and what kinds of consequences it had when it occurred.

Some of the answers I have found are what I originally predicted, but many are not. Even the unexpected findings make a great deal of sense with the advantage of hindsight, but I found them surprising because their implications countered a great deal of the current conventional wisdom. For example, instead of suggesting that what we really need are closer, more tight-knit communities, with denser networks of mutual obligation, my findings suggest that American society would benefit from a larger number of weak ties, that is, relationships that permit looser connections to be maintained on an ongoing basis. Differences of political opinion are indeed more easily maintained and more beneficially aired with one's dentist than with a close friend or family member.

And despite the tremendous negative publicity that currently plagues American businesses, the American workplace is inadvertently performing an important public service simply by establishing a social context in which diverse groups of people are forced into daily interaction with one another. That interaction, as it turns out, often involves discussions of political matters with coworkers and clients who are not of like mind.

As I explain in subsequent chapters, my empirical work in this arena has led me to believe that there are fundamental incompatibilities between theories of participatory democracy and theories of deliberative democracy. *Hearing the Other Side* examines this theme in the context of the contemporary United States. It unearths the social contexts that facilitate conversations across lines of political difference, and the consequences that cross-cutting exposure has for political attitudes and behaviors. Drawing on large quantities of social network data, I illuminate both the benefits and the drawbacks of living in an environment that incorporates differing political viewpoints.

I began this project with the widely shared assumption that face-to-face exposure to differing political views is unquestionably something to be encouraged. But my findings soon convinced me that matters were not so simple as I had supposed. Although diverse political networks foster a better understanding of multiple perspectives on issues and encourage political tolerance, they *discourage* political participation, particularly among those who are averse to conflict. Those with diverse networks refrain from participation in part because of the social awkwardness that accompanies publicly taking a stand that friends or associates may oppose.

When the desire to get along with one another on a day-to-day basis conflicts with the normative dictates of political theory, that inconsistency should give us pause. Many conceptions of civil society blend participatory democracy with deliberative democracy in a seamless fashion, suggesting that the two goals are almost one and the same, with deliberation merely representing a subset of political participation more generally. But based on my findings, it is doubtful that an extremely activist political culture can also be a heavily deliberative one. The best social environment for cultivating political activism is one in which people are surrounded by those who agree with them, people who will reinforce the sense that their own political views are the only right and proper way to proceed. Like-minded people can spur one another on to collective action and promote the kind of passion and enthusiasm that are central to motivating political participation.

Social environments that include close contact among people of differing perspectives may promote a give and take of political ideas, but they are unlikely to foster political fervor. Thus the prospects for truly deliberative encounters may be improving while the prospects for participation and political activism are declining. *Hearing the Other Side* explores the inherent tension between promoting a society with enthusiastically participative citizens and promoting one imbued with tolerance and respect for differences of opinion.

Studying a Moving Target

Face-to-face discussions that cross lines of political difference are central to most conceptions of deliberative democracy.[1] But many of

---

[1] E.g., Fishkin (1991).

the conditions necessary for approximating deliberative ideals such as Habermas's "ideal speech situation"[2] are unlikely to be realized in naturally occurring social contexts.[3] For example, some suggest that in order to qualify, political discussion must take place among citizens of equal status who offer reasonable, carefully constructed, and morally justifiable arguments to one another in a context of mutual respect.[4] Participants must provide reasons that speak to the needs of everyone affected. Such interactions must exclude no one, or at least provide "free and equal access to all,"[5] so that no person has more influence over the process than the next. Strategic behavior is also forbidden. In addition, all participants must be free of the kinds of material deprivations that hinder participation, such as a lack of income or education.[6] And, according to some definitions of deliberation, this process ultimately should lead to a consensus.[7] As a result of these extensive requirements, it is difficult, and perhaps impossible, to "test" a theory of deliberative democracy.

Increasingly, political theorists have been willing to expand their definitions of deliberation beyond this ideal type of rational–critical argument to include more informal forms of conversation such as storytelling, jokes, and greetings and to extend the definition to include emotional as well as rational appeals.[8] Thus even informal discussions are highly valued by contemporary political theory.[9] As Mansbridge notes, "Everyday talk, if not always deliberative, is nevertheless a crucial part of the full deliberative system."[10] Once the bar has been lowered in this fashion, there is obviously more political talk to study, but this still begs the question of whether these political discussions produce consequences of value.[11]

---

[2] Habermas (1989).

[3] Sanders (1997).

[4] Gutmann & Thompson (1996).

[5] Knight & Johnson (1994).

[6] Ackerman & Fishkin (2004); Fishkin (1991); Fishkin (1996).

[7] Macedo (1999) notes that there are many definitions of deliberation, but as Sanders (1997) points out, most have this much in common.

[8] Young (1996). See Mansbridge (1999) for an overview of the conceptual expansion of the "deliberative system."

[9] Gutmann & Thompson (1996) also note this, though it is unclear whether informal everyday deliberation should be held to the same standards as, say, deliberative discourse among officials.

[10] Mansbridge (1999, p. 211).

[11] See Mendelberg (2002) for an excellent review of evidence related to these claims.

In part, the absence of evidence for these benefits is understandable. According to theorists, the benefits of political conversations depend critically on whether such talk reaches the standards necessary to be deemed "deliberation."[12] It is one thing to claim that political conversation has the *potential* to produce beneficial outcomes if it meets a whole variety of unrealized criteria, and yet another to argue that political conversations, as they actually occur, produce meaningful benefits for citizens.[13]

A highly restrictive definition of deliberation obviously presents a quandary for the empirical researcher. If one limits the political communication phenomena worthy of study to those examples of political talk that meet all of the necessary and sufficient conditions collectively invoked by advocates of deliberative democracy, then one is left with a near-empty set of social interactions to study. On the other hand, if one studies an isolated aspect of deliberative processes, one is easily accused of "missing the point" of the larger theory, or of neglecting to operationalize it adequately. To my mind, a third option, namely, avoiding empirical tests of complex theories, is probably least desirable of all. To the extent that empirical research and political theory fail to speak to one another, both fields are impoverished.

Robert Merton famously admonished social scientists to formulate "theories of the middle range," that is, theories not too far removed from on-the-ground, operational research, yet not so narrow and specific as to be irrelevant to larger bodies of theory.[14] Research on deliberative democracy readily illustrates this need. Deliberative democracy is an attractive, broadly encompassing theory of how communicative interaction benefits democracies. But in part *because* of its all-encompassing breadth, attempts to test it empirically often seem lackluster at best, or even irrelevant to the larger theory. The richness of deliberation as a theoretical construct makes empirical research on its tenets pale in comparison. And yet it has not escaped researchers' attention that deliberative theory makes many claims about the benefits of deliberation, claims that, to many scholars' ears, call out for empirical examination.

[12] Habermas (1989).
[13] Conover & Searing (1998).
[14] Merton (1968).

In this research, I take the middle range approach advocated by Merton. I draw on political theory for my expectations, but I study political talk as it occurs (or does not occur) naturally in American social life. Thus rather than examine deliberation per se, that is, a large package of variables all rolled into one concept, I focus on one necessary, though not sufficient, condition in almost all definitions of deliberation: that is, that people be exposed to oppositional political perspectives through political talk. Because this is a minimalist conception of what it means to deliberate, falling far below the requisites of most theorists, I use the term *cross-cutting exposure* or *diverse political networks* so as not to suggest far more than I intend. As Chapter 3 demonstrates, even a minimalist conception does, nonetheless, have some significant consequences for the citizens who engage in it. These benefits are precisely what has been predicted by deliberative theorists.

Theorists may be disappointed with the stripped-down versions of these concepts as they appear in empirical research, and empiricists may chafe at the atypical measures that I have created in an attempt to crudely represent theorists' concepts. But if we are ever to understand what the effects of deliberation are in the real world among ordinary citizens, if we are to move toward a kind of political science in which normative theory and empirical evidence speak to one another, then we need to begin breaking down the various components of this rich concept in order to understand its effects.

Given the difficulties in finding naturally occurring examples of political talk that live up to the high standards of deliberation, some might think it preferable to study carefully constructed public forums, town meetings, or deliberative polls in which the standards of deliberative encounters are at least approximated through extensive advance planning, discussion mediators, rules of engagement, a supply of information and expertise, and so forth. I do not question whether these events have beneficial consequences of various kinds; in fact, my presumption and the preponderance of evidence suggest that they do, particularly for levels of citizen information. But I do question whether such attempts could ever be successfully generalized to large numbers of people and issues. Some see such potential in the Internet, which provides a low-cost means of communicating, but the eventual impact of its use for these purposes remains to be seen.

For most of us, the ideal deliberative encounter is almost other-worldly, bearing little resemblance to the conversations about politics that occur over the water cooler, at the neighborhood bar, or even in our civic groups. The consequences of an ideal deliberative encounter will make little difference if there are few, if any, such exchanges. For this reason I concur with theorists who suggest that everyday talk should receive at least as much theoretical attention as formal deliberation in public arenas designed for these purposes.[15]

Avoiding What's Good for Us?

"Religion and politics," as the old saying goes, "should never be discussed in mixed company." And yet fostering discussions that cross lines of political difference has long been a central concern of political theorists. Political talk is now central to most current conceptions of how democracy functions.[16] More recently, it has also become a cause célèbre for pundits and civic-minded citizens who want to improve the health of American democracy. According to many prominent social theorists, democracy has a future only if "citizens come back out of their bunkers and start talking."[17] The quantity and quality of political conversation have become "a standard for the accomplishment of democracy."[18]

Support for the importance of cross-cutting exposure comes from many quarters. Contemporary social and political theory is rife with the assumption that exposure to conflicting political views benefits the citizens of a democratic polity. For example, Habermas's "ideal speech situation" incorporates the assumption that exposure to dissimilar views will benefit the inhabitants of a public sphere by encouraging greater deliberation and reflection. Exposure to dissimilar views is deemed essential to transcending the parochial nature of personal experience: "In large internally diverse societies, no one's immediate (lifeworld) experience prepares them adequately for political participation."[19]

---

[15] Although other theorists have made similar pleas, Mansbridge (1999) makes this statement most directly.

[16] Schudson (1997).

[17] Gray (1995, p. 1); see also Elshtain (1995); Lasch (1995).

[18] Sanders (1997, p. 347).

[19] Calhoun (1988).

Communitarian theorists further stress the importance of public discourse among people who are different from one another.[20] Political discourse is argued to depend less on the amount of political talk, and more on the quality of those conversations and the diversity of views represented. Calhoun concurs: "Democratic public discourse does not depend on pre-existing harmony or similarity among citizens... but rather on the ability to create meaningful discourses across lines of difference."[21]

Perhaps the most often cited proponent of communication across lines of difference is John Stuart Mill, who pointed out how a lack of contact with oppositional viewpoints diminishes the prospects for a public sphere: "If the opinion is right, they are deprived of the opportunity of exchanging error for truth; if wrong, they lose what is almost as great a benefit, the clearer perception and livelier impression of truth produced by its collision with error."[22] Likewise, Habermas assumes that exposure to dissimilar views will benefit the inhabitants of a public sphere by encouraging greater interpersonal deliberation and intrapersonal reflection.[23]

According to Arendt, exposure to conflicting political views also plays an integral role in encouraging "enlarged mentality," that is, the capacity to form an opinion "by considering a given issue from different viewpoints, by making present to my mind the standpoints of those who are absent.... The more people's standpoints I have present in my mind while I am pondering a given issue, and the better I can imagine how I would feel and think if I were in their place, the stronger will be my capacity for representative thinking and the more valid my final conclusions, my opinion."[24] Interactions with others of differing views are assumed to be "essential for us to comprehend and to come to appreciate the perspective of others."[25]

Awareness of rationales for oppositional views is a particularly important type of political knowledge because of its close ties to legitimacy. Cross-cutting exposure is assumed to promote greater awareness

[20] E.g., Barber (1984); Bellah, Madsen, Sullivan, Swidler, & Tipton (1985).
[21] Calhoun (1988, p. 220).
[22] Mill (1956, p. 21) [1859].
[23] Habermas (1989).
[24] Arendt (1968, p. 241).
[25] Benhabib (1992, p. 140).

of oppositional views because no individual person thinking in isolation can foresee the variety of perspectives through which political issues may be perceived.[26] Thus political deliberation "teaches citizens to see things they had previously overlooked, including the views of others."[27] The purpose served by conveying rationales for oppositional views is to help render the ultimate decision or policy legitimate in the eyes of others.[28] If rationales are not made public, the losers in a given controversy will not know what reasons or arguments the winners judged to be stronger in deciding the merits of the case: "Hence discussion rather than private deliberation would be necessary to 'put on the table' the various reasons and arguments that different individuals had in mind, and thus to ensure that no one could see the end result as arbitrary rather than reasonable and justifiable, even if not what he or she happened to see as *most* justifiable."[29]

To summarize, hearing the other side has long been considered important for democratic citizens. Advocates of deliberative democracy stress the importance of communication across lines of difference, and the existence of differing views is arguably the raison d'être for political deliberation. Unfortunately empirical work has fallen far behind political theory in this realm. Only recently have scholars begun investigations of where and with what consequences people interact with those whose political views differ from their own in the contexts of their day-to-day lives.

But if everyone is so deliriously enthusiastic about the potential benefits of exposing people to oppositional political perspectives, then what exactly is the problem? Given the unusually strong consensus surrounding its assumed value, one would assume this activity to be widespread. Why don't people go home, to church, or to work and discuss politics with their non–like-minded friends or acquaintances?

Social network studies have long suggested that likes talk to likes; in other words, people tend to selectively expose themselves to people who do not challenge their view of the world.[30] Network survey

---

[26] Manin (1987).

[27] Ibid., p. 351.

[28] Ibid.

[29] Fearon (1998, p. 62).

[30] In addition, Green, Visser, & Tetlock (2000) describe several ways that people who anticipate exposure to oppositional political views will avoid such encounters.

after network survey has shown that people talk more to those who are like them than to those who are not, and political agreement is no exception to this general pattern.[31] Moreover, many people do not have much desire to engage in political debate to begin with, even the informal variety. Exposure to diverse political viewpoints may be widely advocated in theory, but it is much less popular in actual practice. In this sense, the extent to which people are exposed to oppositional views demonstrates some of the same patterns as exposure to diversity along other dimensions, such as race and class. While diversity is a much-lauded public goal in the aggregate, few individual people live their everyday lives so as to maximize their exposure to difference.

What Is Meant by Diversity? Some Definitional Issues

Discussions of how social environments affect citizens are frequently hindered by a confusion borne of inconsistent terminology. The term *context*, for example, has a colloquial usage that includes the environment, but it is not specific as to what kind of social milieu the writer has in mind. Further, since most people inhabit multiple social contexts – the home, the workplace, the neighborhood, the city, state, and so forth – it makes little sense to talk about the influence of context as if it were one identifiable unit for each individual. In some cases, the characteristics of these contexts are used as surrogates for characteristics of the person's social network or the social influence processes exerting influence on him or her.

For purposes of this book, I use the term *network* to refer specifically to the people with whom a given person communicates on a direct, one-to-one basis. Network members are clearly part of a person's communication environment. *Contexts*, on the other hand, refer to larger entities (neighborhoods, workplaces, cities, etc.) whose characteristics are typically known to the researcher strictly in aggregate form and are known to the individual only in piecemeal form. The communicative influence of social contexts on individuals flows *through* the people who are part of a person's network. An individual's network thus

---

[31] See Cotton (1985) for a review of evidence on selective exposure to communications more generally.

may include people known through a variety of social contexts (work, school, neighborhood, family), and the individual's sense of his or her larger social context may be inferred, correctly or incorrectly, from network members known through that context.

Because this book is focused on hearing the other side, my central concern is with the extent to which people's networks involve like-minded versus non–like-minded discussion partners. Inevitably then, terms such as *diversity*, *homogeneity* and *heterogeneity* crop up. Unlike many treatments of these topics, my concern is strictly with *political* difference. This emphasis is not intended to disparage the importance of other types of heterogeneity or diversity, but it does serve to bring us closer to what is of interest in studies of political speech – how people come to express and listen to oppositional political views. By studying the expression of oppositional political views (as opposed to political conversations among those who are *demographically* dissimilar), I bring the evidence closer to the essence of why diverse points of view are protected – because we believe it is valuable for people to hear them.

The principle of diversity has been much touted and widely celebrated in the contemporary United States. But what is meant by diversity or heterogeneity in people's social environments may vary. In sociology, the study of diverse social contexts is linked to urban sociology and the study of cities. But consider diversity–heterogeneity in the form that Robert Ezra Park first ascribed it to cities: "a mosaic of little worlds that touch but do not interpenetrate."[32] In this depiction of diversity, "individuals' own networks, located inside those little 'worlds' – are not diverse. In fact, they are probably less diverse than the personal networks of comparable rural people."[33]

For this reason, urban versus rural social contexts are less important to the story I tell than the extent to which political difference actually "happens" to people in the course of their everyday lives. But Park's "mosaic" usefully reminds us that highly diverse political contexts, and even highly competitive contexts such as division of the United States into roughly half Republicans and half Democrats, are no guarantee that people hear the other side in the course of their day-to-day lives.

[32] Park (1967, p. 40).
[33] Fischer (1999, p. 216).

These two kinds of diversity – at the level at which it is experienced by an individual, and as a characteristic of an aggregate – may even be at odds. As sociologist Claude Fischer suggests, "As the society becomes more diverse, the individuals' own social networks become less diverse. More than ever, perhaps, the child of an affluent professional family may live, learn, and play with only similar children; the elderly factory worker may retire and relax only among other aged members of the working class."[34]

Available data make it difficult to establish whether and to what extent the United States is trending toward more politically homogeneous lifestyle enclaves. But census data make demographic diversity easier to track than political characteristics. In the case of demographics, many agree that subcultures organized around class, religion, lifestyles, and other interests are on the rise.[35] To the extent that trends of this nature produce more politically homogeneous geographic areas, they may well affect levels of diversity in citizens' social networks. Political homogeneity in this case would be a result of de facto selective exposure. As discussed in Chapter 2, relatively few people think explicitly about the political climate when choosing a place to live, but lifestyle choices may serve as surrogates for political views, producing a similar end result.

The level of heterogeneity in a person's political *network* is not necessarily the same as the heterogeneity of the social *context* he or she inhabits. One can certainly influence the other, but hearing the other side takes place at the level of discussants within a network rather than within some larger, aggregate social context. For this reason, my research is focused on pragmatic, *experiential diversity* that occurs in people's everyday political experience, that is, the people with whom they actually discuss political matters. From this perspective, political diversity is something experienced at the individual level, a characteristic of an individual's life experiences and contacts. Although one can certainly aggregate individuals' experiences of this kind so as to characterize experiential diversity within a large population, this is a different conceptualization of diversity from those characterizing that

[34] Ibid., p. 219.
[35] For examples of these kinds of claims, see Frey (1995).

same population as politically diverse because it includes people of oppositional and perhaps extreme political perspectives – people who may or may not have contact with one another.

Given this focus, when I use the terms *homogeneity* and *heterogeneity* in this study, they refer to the extent to which contact within political networks reinforces preexisting beliefs or challenges them, respectively. From this perspective, *diversity* refers not to a broad range of differences within an aggregate, nor to the extent that each differs from the other within the aggregate, but rather to the extent that a given person is exposed to those of oppositional views versus those of like mind. For purposes of the kinds of benefits that hearing the other side is supposed to provide, what is most important about network composition is whether one's discussants incorporate oppositional views or whether the network is dominated by like-minded discussants.

A Departure from Studying Political Preferences

The evidence in this book is taken from a variety of social network surveys fielded between 1992 and 2000. Most studies of political networks have focused on elections, and these are no exceptions. They were initially designed with the goal of understanding how social influence occurs in political networks, and particularly how it shapes an individual's vote preference. Within political science, this has been the central focus of studies that have gone to the considerable time and expense of systematically assessing the qualities of Americans' political networks.

Two types of social influence dominate contemporary thinking about what happens when people discuss political topics. When those of dissimilar views interact, conformity pressures are argued to encourage those holding minority viewpoints to adopt the prevailing attitude. When those of like mind come together, the feared outcome is polarization: that is, people within homogeneous networks may be reinforced so that they hold the same viewpoints, only more strongly.

However, social influence is not the only, nor even necessarily the most important, consequence of being exposed to others' views through informal communication. Even Solomon Asch, whose reputation was built on studying conformity and its perils, acknowledged the capacity for something beneficial, something other than social influence, to result from exposure to oppositional views:

> The other is capable of arousing in me a doubt that would otherwise not occur to me. The clash of views generates events of far-reaching importance. I am induced to take up a particular standpoint, to view my own action as another views it or as the action of another person, and, conversely, to view another's action as my own. Now I have within me two standpoints, my own and that of the other; both are now part of my way of thinking. In this way the limitations of my individual thinking are transcended by including the thoughts of others. I am now open to more alternatives than my own unaided comprehension would make possible.[36]

In an important sense this research is about the flip side of these well-known studies of persuasive influence. Instead of studying where social influence occurs, this study focuses on situations in which it does *not* occur, examining the value that derives from engaging in conversation with those who are *unsuccessful* at persuading us to hold like-minded views but nonetheless successful in making us acknowledge the value of alternatives, in making us empathize with the perspectives of those who disagree. Ultimately, cross-cutting exposure should enable citizens to perceive political controversies as legitimate differences of opinion.

One would think that political discourse would be richer for incorporating a sensitivity to oppositional political perspectives, but it might also be more persuasive as a result. Interestingly, the essay portion of the new Scholastic Aptitude Test (SAT) given to college-bound high school students rewards taking a firm stance in the persuasive essay and sticking to that stance throughout. Acknowledging the legitimacy of oppositional arguments is warned against in a popular test preparation book: "What's important is that you take a position and state how you feel. It is not important what other people might think, just what you think."[37] But as one critic of the current persuasive essay suggests, "It is hard to communicate if the only side of an argument you can hear is your own."[38]

---

[36] Asch (1952, pp. 131–132).
[37] Excerpt from Kaplan's New SAT test-preparation book, as cited in Hulbert (2005, p. 16).
[38] Hulbert (1994, p. 16).

Deliberative versus Participatory Democracy?

I began this project as an effort to document empirically some of the unsubstantiated benefits of politically diverse social networks. Inspired by the enthusiasm for deliberative democracy, I set out to test what seemed to be some of the most plausible positive outcomes, as they might occur in naturalistic settings. Although I substantiated some of these benefits, the relationships that I did not anticipate made the project far more puzzling. It only slowly dawned on me that what I was seeing challenged some of the more basic, fundamental assumptions in theories of deliberative and participatory democracy.

To introduce the reader to the source of this dilemma, I start out slowly in Chapter 2, introducing the descriptive characteristics of cross-cutting exposure in network dyads. What kind of people are likely to have politically diverse networks, the kind that would naturally challenge their own views? Chapter 2 makes the further point that much of what has been assumed about the prevalence of disagreement in Americans' networks is not as rosy as it first appears. Moreover, relative to people in many other countries, Americans maintain highly homogeneous political networks.

In Chapter 3, I test three common assertions about beneficial effects of cross-cutting exposure. I draw on multiple studies to examine the impact of heterogeneous versus homogeneous networks of political discussion on individuals' awareness of legitimate rationales for oppositional viewpoints, on their awareness of rationales for their own viewpoints, and on levels of political tolerance. Further, I analyze the important role that civility plays in deriving benefits from cross-cutting political networks.

In Chapter 4, I link the study of cross-cutting political networks to studies of cross-pressures, a long-dormant area of research in American politics. I find that diverse political discussion networks have important drawbacks as well as benefits.

Finally, in Chapter 5, I synthesize the contradictory implications from the previous chapters. If neither homogeneous political networks nor heterogeneous networks are without deleterious consequences, what kind of social environment is best for the citizens of a democratic polity?

The thesis of this book is that theories of participatory democracy are in important ways inconsistent with theories of deliberative democracy. The best possible social environment for purposes of either one of these two goals would naturally undermine the other. In my mind's eye, I suppose I had always had great difficulty visualizing these two theories in a single image. Like the cover of this book, the pinnacle of participatory democracy was, to my mind, a throng of highly politically active citizens carrying signs, shouting slogans, and cheering on the speeches of their political leaders. On days without such events, they worked together in a dingy basement stuffing envelopes for a direct mail campaign, wrote letters to their political representatives urging support of their views, canvassed door to door, or planned fund-raising events to buy television and radio time to promote their candidates or causes.

This was participatory democracy as I had known it. There was a level of enthusiasm and passion borne of shared purpose, and a camaraderie that emerged from the sheer amount of time spent together. Discussions among those who shared political views helped spur one another on to still higher levels of involvement, rallied the "troops" in times of discouragement, and buoyed spirits among the like-minded, convincing them that win or lose, promoting their candidate or cause was truly worth their time and efforts. It was the right thing to do; it was politics as a way of life, to paraphrase Dewey.[39]

Deliberation, even in the minimalist form in which it occurs in the course of everyday people's lives, was unlikely to occur in such a homogeneous setting. While people would surely talk about politics while stuffing envelopes, and they might even have minor disagreements over minor technical matters involving political issues, they would be secure in the knowledge that their basic values and political goals were shared. These partisans could easily be admired for their political knowledge and their activism, but they would be rather like what John Stuart Mill called "one eyed men," that is, people whose perspectives were partial and thus inevitably somewhat narrow. As Mill acknowledged, "If they saw more, they probably would not see so keenly, nor so eagerly pursue one course of enquiry."[40]

---

[39] Barber (1984).
[40] Mill (1969, p. 94).

Given its insistence on cross-cutting political conversation, informal deliberation had to be found elsewhere if at all – perhaps at serious dinner parties, maybe at work, in the neighborhood, or at meetings. The tone as well as the context associated with deliberation seemed completely inappropriate for most participatory settings. The prototypical deliberative encounter – a calm, rational exchange of views in near-monotone voices – did not convey the passionate enthusiasm that I associated with political participation. Could deliberation and participation really be part and parcel of the same goal? Would the same kind of social and political environment conducive to diverse political networks also promote participation? The chapters that follow attempt to answer these questions.

2

Encountering Mixed Political Company

With Whom and in What Context?

In a 2004 Miss Manners column, a reader wrote in with the following question:

Dear Miss Manners:

In this election year, I am struck by a barrier to participation in the world's most famous democracy – that being Americans' reluctance to consider political discourse to be polite conversation.

In most parts of the world, it might be considered far more engaging dinner conversation to contrast the qualities of candidates for office than, say, to discuss the less savory sorts of reality television.

I find the rigor with which reasoned political discourse – or even discussion of complex news topics – is quashed as if it's a threat to future generations' participation in our communities. I certainly grew up with animated (but cordial) political discussion in many formal and informal venues.

Yet broach the subject of an election at most dinner tables or cocktail parties and it's as though you were discussing something shameful or utterly beyond proper behavior.

My European friends are actually shocked at the lack of casual discourse on political matters here, and frankly so am I.

Could you please elaborate as to the proper place of free speech in mixed company?

Miss Manners responds:

You mean people of mixed political opinions, who are going to feel free to say what they think about the morals and intelligence of people who disagree with them about politics (or sex or religion, which are also banned from the dinner table)?

Miss Manners suggests you try bringing up a topic from each of these areas – for example, the death penalty, same-sex marriage, or abortion – and see how much polite, cordial and reasoned discourse you provoke.

She would be only too happy to welcome the return of substantive conversation at dinner parties; goodness knows she is weary of hearing people talk about the food. But conversation requires listening respectfully to others and engaging in polite give-and-take, rather than making speeches and imputing others' motives and judgment.

Unless you are sure you are among those who know how to express their opinions politely and listen to others' respectfully, Miss Manners suggests you be grateful for those discussions of reality television.[1]

The status of political conversation in mixed company is clearly quite different within academe than it is outside it. In academic circles it is celebrated and encouraged, whereas in the so-called real world it is seen as not only unnecessary, but at times even counterproductive. If as little conversation across lines of political difference occurs as Miss Manners recommends, then it would hardly be worth a book. But because such conversation does occur – though certainly in varying degrees within the networks of various types of people – it is important to sort out its benefits and drawbacks, to be neither wholly dismissive of its potential to contribute to the political process in everyday practice nor wholly accepting of the many virtues attributed to it in theory.

The ongoing popularity of theories of deliberative democracy has prompted scholars to consider whether political discussion is more than just another form of political involvement. Whereas for years it was classified by the American National Election Studies as one of many indicators of "political participation," its contemporary status in academe is clearly more eminent than it once was. Rightly or wrongly, contemporary social scientists grant political discussion a more elevated status than forms of participation such as displaying bumper stickers or donating money to a campaign. Money may be dirty, but political discourse is golden.

To justify studying cross-cutting exposure as a concept in its own right, we first need to be assured that political talk, and cross-cutting

---

[1] Martin (2004). I thank Marci McCoy for bringing this example to my attention.

political talk in particular, is more than just another indicator of something already well studied under another term. We need to know, for example, that we can discriminate between the extent of cross-cutting political conversation and closely related concepts such as political involvement, social capital, or general political discussion. Toward that end, I focus this chapter at the descriptive level, sketching a preliminary portrait of the relationships, the social contexts, and the people who engage in conversations with those whose political viewpoints oppose their own.

What characterizes those exposed to cross-cutting political talk? Is it the same group of people who participate in politics more generally? To be sure, the extent to which people talk about politics must be partly a function of levels of political interest and activity; that much should be obvious. But the answer to the question of who engages in *cross-cutting* political conversation is more complex because this activity is a function of both the characteristics and interests of individuals and the social contexts in which individuals find themselves. To some extent it is individually controlled, but it is also environmentally imposed. Does it correspond with what others have dubbed "social capital"? Where and with whom do cross-cutting conversations originate? Only after establishing that mixed political company should be considered a concept in its own right do I turn to the consequences of political conversation across lines of difference as the focus of subsequent chapters.

Sources of Evidence

To get a sense of how Americans become engaged in cross-cutting political conversations, I relied on several representative national surveys that included information on Americans' networks of political discussion. In each case a random sample of Americans was interviewed, and they were asked an extensive battery of questions about the people with whom they talked about politics. Although there are minor differences from survey to survey, the studies are remarkably consistent in the story they tell.

I use the surveys for illustrative purposes in Chapter 2. In subsequent chapters I tackle the messier business of establishing cause and effect relationships between cross-cutting exposure and the many consequences hypothesized to flow from it. The empirical evidence in the book relies primarily, though not exclusively, on data from three representative national surveys of Americans and their political networks: The 1992 American component of the Cross National Election Project (CNEP) survey, the 2000 American National Election Study (NES), and a 1996 survey funded by the Spencer Foundation and gathered by the University of Wisconsin-Madison Survey Research Center. Two of these three studies were designed for purposes of studying social influence during an election campaign; the third was designed explicitly for purposes of examining exposure to oppositional political views.

Technical details on each of these studies can be found elsewhere.[2] Their similarities were more numerous than their differences: all three were representative national samples that included a "discussant generator," that is, a question that served as a basis for getting the respondent to name people in his or her network. The CNEP asked about people with whom they talked about "important matters" for the first four discussants and about an election campaign discussant for the fifth, whereas the Spencer Foundation and NES surveys focused explicitly on *political* discussants. Previous comparisons of name generators suggest that an explicitly political frame produces more nonrelatives and discussants who are weak ties,[3] thus making the Spencer and NES surveys more likely to generate discussants who are politically dissimilar to the main respondents.

For each discussant named, these items were followed by a battery of questions tapping the frequency with which the respondent talked about politics with each discussant, as well as features of this relationship such as how they knew one another and how close their relationship was. The three studies differed in the maximum number of discussants that could be named: the Spencer survey was limited to three, the National Election Study to four, and the CNEP survey allowed up to five.

All of these surveys also allowed some means of distinguishing whether the respondent and each of his or her discussants were of like mind, of oppositional political views, or neither. In the NES

[2] For details on the CNEP American study see Beck, Dalton, & Huckfeldt (1995). For details on the Spencer Foundation survey, see Mutz & Martin (2001); Mutz (2002a); Mutz (2002b). For details on the National Election Studies data, see Burns, Kinder, & the National Election Studies (2003).
[3] Huckfeldt & Sprague (1995b).

survey only one indicator was available to make this assessment, a comparison of the respondent's vote preference and the discussant's vote preference. Other surveys included as many as five indicators of exposure to oppositional views such as the frequency with which he or she disagreed with the views of the political discussants that were named, whether the respondent perceived his or her views to be generally the same as or different from the discussants', and whether the discussant generally shared or opposed his or her political views. Some also were asked about the discussant's party identification, and these questions were combined with information on the respondent's own partisanship to form additional indicators of political similarity and difference.

Given that political discussion of all types is likely to characterize those more politically interested, knowledgeable, and involved, measures of these predispositions were required in each of these surveys in order to disentangle the impact of general political involvement from the impact of exposure to oppositional views. For example, it was important to distinguish between effects due to the *extent* of political discussion and effects due to discussion of politics with those who are not of like mind. To the extent that the impact of exposure to dissonant views is unique, and its effects are not attributable to political discussion more generally, or to political interest and involvement, then the benefits suggested by many theorists gain support.

Analyses drawn from these three main surveys were supplemented with experimental evidence, data from the World Values Surveys,[4] and data from additional countries involved in the CNEP surveys.[5] In addition, the American component of the CNEP survey provided additional insight by including both *perceptions* of discussants' views and independent assessments of the extent of political disagreement made possible by a separate survey of the respondents' discussants for whom contact information was available.

Each of these studies had different strengths and weaknesses. For example, although the Spencer survey had a relatively small sample,

---

[4] See Inglehart, Basanez, Diez-Medrano, Halman, & Luijkx (2004).
[5] See Beck, Dalton, & Huckfeldt (1995) for details on the CNEP American Study. The World Values data for these comparisons came from ICPSR #3975. See also Inglehart and colleagues (2004) for more on the World Values data.

it provided tremendous depth of information about the extent of exposure to political disagreement. Moreover, providing multiple indicators of the dependent variable made it possible to create an index that offered a more reliable measure of the extent to which a given source provided exposure to oppositional views. Unfortunately, this survey included only one item tapping political participation. The CNEP study, in contrast, included more participation measures, plus a question addressing time of presidential vote decision, but it incorporated less information on exposure to political difference within the respondent's network. Nonetheless both surveys represent an improvement in the operationalization of some key concepts.[6]

Despite its limited information on cross-cutting exposure, a unique strength of the CNEP was that it allowed comparisons with other countries on some of its survey items. In addition, it provided a means of assessing the extent of accuracy in respondents' self-reports on the political leanings of their political discussants.[7] Because the American CNEP data included independent reports of candidate choice by the discussants themselves, the extent of projection of their own views onto their discussants is known. Only 12 percent of the respondent–discussant dyads showed potential evidence of projection of the respondents' own political views onto the discussant, the main source of distortion on respondent perceptions. A full 78 percent of respondents' perceptions were accurate reports of the discussants' views; the remaining 9 percent were situations in which perceptual errors were made in the direction of a candidate *other* than the respondent's favored one.[8] Only 8 percent of dyads involved perceptual errors in which the

---

[6] The traditional approach to studying cross-pressures, for instance, simply *assumed* cross-cutting exposure based on membership in combinations of particular religious, economic, occupational, age, or racial categories that may (or may not) have been central to an individual's social network; that may (or may not) have represented oppositional political perspectives; and that may (or may not) have exerted cross-pressures on respondents through political communication. I elaborate on these problems and their consequences in the discussion in Chapter 4.

[7] See, e.g., Huckfeldt & Sprague (1995a). Although respondents are likely to perceive somewhat greater agreement in their networks than actually exists, it is their *perceptions* of their discussants' views that should shape whatever consequences flow from the heterogeneity or homogeneity of the network. For this reason perceptual measures are preferable to assessments drawn from the perspectives of discussants. Of course, measures obtained directly from discussants may be subject to inaccuracies as well.

[8] Mutz & Martin (2001).

respondent preferred one candidate and erroneously claimed that the discussant preferred the same one. The remainder were cases in which a neutral discussant was erroneously perceived to favor the respondent's own candidate.

Despite these relatively high levels of accuracy in respondent perceptions, some might consider the discussants' self-reports superior to the perceptions of them provided by the respondents. However, for purposes of operationalizing what is likely to influence the respondent, it makes little sense to argue that discussants' views will influence the respondent even when these views have not been clearly communicated to the respondent. Although the choice of which measure to use makes little difference in these particular data, arguing that respondents will experience cross-pressures to the extent that they *recognize* that their network members hold differing political views makes more theoretical sense.

What Kind of Relationships?

What kinds of relationships allow political conversation with those who do not share one's own views? To examine this question, I began by using the Spencer Foundation survey, which provided extensive information on the extent of like-mindedness in respondents' networks. Using pairs of survey respondents and each of their network members with whom they talk politics, each relationship was characterized according to its extent of political agreement or disagreement.[9] To make these scales more intuitively meaningful, higher scores signified a greater extent of perceived political disagreement in the relationship, and lower scores signified a higher degree of political agreement. Relationships that involved neither agreement nor disagreement had no net effect on the scales. On average, the measure of cross-cutting exposure is always a negative score, thus indicating that political discussants tend more toward political agreement than disagreement. This pattern is not at all surprising; in fact, it would be extremely surprising if it

[9] In the Spencer survey, for example, five different questions were used to characterize the heterogeneity or homogeneity of each of these relationships (see Mutz & Martin 2001). These scores were centered on 0 so that positive scores connote the extent of exposure to disagreement, and negative scores signify that the relationship predominantly involves exposure to agreement.

were otherwise. Previous research on social and political networks has repeatedly documented the tendency toward homophily, that is, for likes to talk to likes.

Although birds of a feather do tend to flock together, people also have conversations with those of oppositional political views. Some degree of political diversity exists in many people's networks. Variation in the extent to which a network reinforces or challenges a respondent's views runs from a wholly reinforcing, like-minded network to one that includes some who are nonpartisan, to a network comprised mainly of nonpartisans, to one in which those of oppositional views dominate. The variation along this continuum serves as the central independent variable in the analyses documented in this book.

What kind of relationship is best for sustaining conversations across lines of political difference? The persistence of political disagreement owes a great deal to "weak ties,"[10] or "loose connections,"[11] that is, relationships that are not of the close, intimate variety. When one examines the individual respondent–discussant relationships involved in political talk, one can see that the extent of political disagreement in a relationship steadily decreases as the intimacy of the relationship increases. As shown in the line marked by diamonds in Figure 2.1, it is those relationships characterized as "mere acquaintances," rather than as friends, that are most likely to involve political disagreement.

The second line in Figure 2.1 makes an equally important point. Not surprisingly, political discussion becomes more frequent as relationships become more intimate. So although weak ties are more likely to involve people with whom one disagrees, political conversations with these people will occur more sporadically than those with friends and family members. The extent of disagreement in these pairs and the frequency of political talk that occurs in them are inversely related, thus creating an unfortunate Catch-22. Closer relationships may breed more frequent political conversations, but in that case they will, in all likelihood, be among those who agree. Casual acquaintances, on the other hand, are likely places for political disagreement, but these conversations are unlikely to occur on a frequent basis. Given the extent to which the political network deck appears to be stacked against

[10] See Granovetter (1973).
[11] Wuthnow (1998).

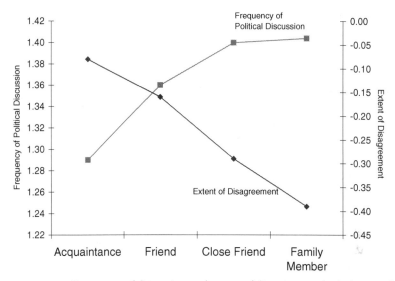

FIGURE 2.1. Frequency of discussion and extent of disagreement by intimacy of relationship. (Note: Data from Spencer Foundation Survey, *n* = 1,700 dyads.)

extensive discussions involving people of nonlike minds, one wonders where and with whom cross-cutting political talk takes place.

First, where do those of nonlike mind meet one another? Respondents were asked where they met each of the people with whom they reported talking politics, and they were asked about up to three possible people. Responses for each dyad were then coded into a number of categories, including meeting through mutual friends and associates, meeting through relatives, growing up together, attending the same place of worship, living in the same neighborhood, or belonging to the same formal groups or organizations.

The percentages shown at the top of each bar in Figure 2.2 indicate what proportion of dyads originate in each of a variety of social contexts, excluding ones in which the two people are relatives.[12] The largest percentage of dyads know one another because they work together (39 percent), or because friends or relatives had introduced

[12] The plurality of discussant pairs know one another because they are related (28%), but Figure 2.2 is focused on nonrelative discussants because of the need to understand the origins of cross-cutting discussions in particular. Members of families are indeed politically similar, though interestingly they are less homogeneous than members of the same congregation.

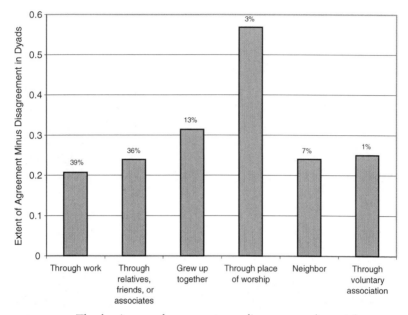

FIGURE 2.2. The dominance of agreement over disagreement, by social context of relationship's origin. (Note: Spencer Foundation Survey, dyad-level data.)

them to one another (36 percent). Places of worship and all other voluntary associations combine to account for just under 5 percent of political discussants, thus suggesting that these social contexts are not exactly hot spots for the development of relationships that lead to political discourse. Likewise, neighborhoods account for a mere 7 percent, despite the fact that they are also a widely studied context for political discussion.

However, as indicated by the height of the bars in Figure 2.2, whether people talk politics with many or relatively few people in a given context can be misleading as an indicator of how likely they are to be exposed to political disagreement in that particular context. The height of the bars in Figure 2.2 represents the extent of disagreement minus the extent of disagreement on average for dyads met through each social context. The positive scores suggest that *all* of these social contexts have more agreement than disagreement in their dyads, but the extent to which agreement dominates disagreement varies. Conversations with those known though a place of worship, for example, are overwhelmingly among those of like mind, and provide the most reinforcement of existing views. Discussants met through relatives and those who grew up together are also relatively similar to the main respondents in their political views. Those dyads formed through the workplace, in contrast, are least likely to involve conversations that involve political agreement.[13] The relatively high percentage of dyads formed there, combined with the relatively low likelihood of homogeneity, makes the workplace a promising venue for cross-cutting political discourse.

Although one might quibble with these categories – meeting through friends and relatives is not, after all, a specific social context – the general lesson of these findings is nonetheless clear and consistent. If one wants to harness the power of social networks for the kinds of purposes envisioned by advocates of deliberative democracy, voluntary associations and neighborhoods are probably *not* the best places to start. Although one could certainly facilitate conversations at the level of neighborhoods and local organizations, political disagreement is greatly underrepresented in the kinds of conversations that are likely to occur voluntarily in these contexts. Of the various social contexts identified, the workplace appears most promising as a site for cross-cutting political conversations.

What Kind of People?

Understanding the kinds of relationships that incorporate political disagreement is only part of the story. To get a sense of what kind of *people* engage in cross-cutting political conversation, I needed an individual-level measure of the extent of cross-cutting exposure, preferably one that took into account the degree of political similarity versus dissimilarity of the discussant, as well as the frequency of political talk between each discussant and the main respondent. To do this I first standardized the measures of extent of agreement versus disagreement so that the average mean across all dyads, regardless of order mentioned, was set to 0. Because the scales used to tap agreement–disagreement were relative rather than absolute scales, a standardized index of similarity versus dissimilarity effectively ranked dyads from most to least similar

---

[13] See Mutz & Mondak (1998).

in political views. The dyad-level measures also were weighted to take into account the relative frequency of talk within each dyad.

To create measures of each individual respondent's exposure to cross-cutting views, these indicators were summed across however many discussants a given respondent had. Thus a discussant in total agreement with the main respondent would push the respondent's cross-cutting exposure balance in a negative direction, and a discussant with divergent views would push the score in a positive direction, and all the more so if discussion between the respondent and discussant occurred frequently. This combined measure is referred to as the individual's *extent of exposure* to cross-cutting political discussion. All else being equal, those with higher levels of cross-cutting exposure should enjoy more of the benefits ascribed to this activity than those with lower levels of cross-cutting exposure.

One logical conjecture would be to expect this form of political behavior to be much like any other. In other words, it would be disproportionately the province of well-educated, high-income populations. Indeed, the frequency of general political discussion tracks closely with these characteristics of high socioeconomic status. But the correlates of cross-cutting conversation are strikingly different. As shown in Figure 2.3, there are clear patterns of difference with respect to race, income, and education, but they are not in the usual directions. Nonwhites are significantly *more* likely to engage in cross-cutting political conversation than whites. And as income increases, the frequency of disagreeable conversations *declines*. Exposure to disagreement is *highest* among those who have completed less than a high school degree and lowest among those who have attended graduate school. Finally, age is also related to exposure to cross-cutting views, but in a curvilinear fashion. The youngest and oldest tend to have higher levels of cross-cutting exposure; those in the middle find it relatively rare.

Talking about politics a lot, and talking about politics with those of oppositional views characterize very different parts of the population. Of course, the relationships illustrated in Figure 2.3 are purely bivariate ones, and they are not intended to suggest that these characteristics are necessarily *causes* of greater or lesser cross-cutting exposure. Still, it is clear that low levels of cross-cutting exposure characterize those who generally have higher status in life: whites, those with high incomes and high levels of formal education. The same characteristics that give

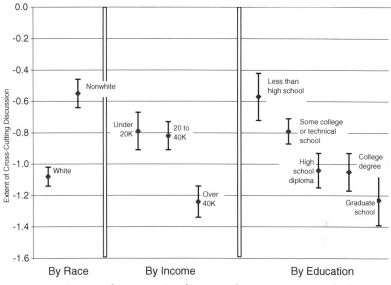

FIGURE 2.3. Extent of cross-cutting discussion by race, income, and education. (Note: Spencer Foundation Survey, *n* = 780 respondents.)

people more control over their lives in general also give them more control over with whom they associate. To the extent that people see their lives as easier or more comfortable if they are surrounded by like-minded others, high socio-economic status allows some people to achieve that end more than others.

What Kind of Politics?

For opinionated citizens, the persistence of political disagreement is something of a mystery. As Schauer muses,

It is a continuing source of astonishment for me that such a small percentage of even my soundest opinions command widespread assent. Indeed, my only source of solace in this is the knowledge that most others experience life in similar ways and thus must confront daily the obtuseness of their fellow citizens. For many of us, the resistance of other members of the community to even our strongest arguments is a continuing and puzzling frustration.[14]

---

[14] Schauer (1999, p. 17).

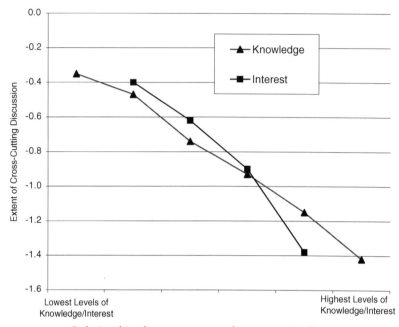

FIGURE 2.4. Relationships between extent of cross-cutting discussion in network and political knowledge and political interest. (Note: Spencer Foundation Survey, *n* = 780 respondents.)

Schauer's tongue-in-cheek description of a common political lament is all too familiar. Quite often there is fundamental disbelief in the notion that reasonable people can disagree on political matters. Hibbing and Theiss-Morse found that this was a recurrent theme in public opinion as well.[15] The answers are obvious and we all agree on them. So what is wrong with all of those *other* people? Diverse networks should play an important role in increasing awareness and understanding of the opposition. But are the politically interested and involved exposed to cross-cutting discourse?

As shown in Figure 2.4, those most knowledgeable about and interested in politics are *not* the people most exposed to oppositional political viewpoints. The dominance of like-minded over oppositional voices increases as political knowledge increases.[16] Likewise, as self-reported

[15] Hibbing & Theiss-Morse (2002).
[16] By *political knowledge* here I mean as measured by a standard battery of civics knowledge questions; see Delli Carpini & Keeter (1996).

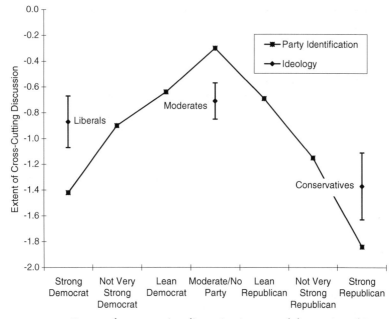

FIGURE 2.5. Extent of cross-cutting discussion in network by partisanship and ideology. (Note: Spencer Foundation Survey, $n = 780$ respondents.)

levels of political interest increase, the extent of exposure to disagreement also declines. In short, it is the "good citizens" of American politics who appear most wanting by this criterion, and thus who are most troubled by the lack of consensus in the broader political world. Those who are highly politically involved are not as likely to expose themselves to cross-cutting political perspectives.

Further, as Figure 2.5 illustrates with its pronounced curvilinear relationship, cross-cutting political networks are more common among political moderates. Those who consider themselves liberals or conservatives and those who self-identify as partisans on either end of the spectrum are less likely to be exposed to cross-cutting political communication. In addition, there is a significant asymmetry to the patterns in Figure 2.5 such that being a strong Republican or a conservative corresponds to a lower level of cross-cutting exposure than being a strong Democrat or a liberal. This finding appears regularly across social network studies. Republicans' networks tend to be more politically homogeneous. But the overall pattern in Figure 2.5 suggests that partisans and ideologues on *both* ends of the spectrum have less exposure to those who have oppositional views than do those in the middle.

When I first encountered this curvilinear pattern I assumed it must have something to do with apolitical people in the central categories of this scale. But further analyses demonstrated that it did not matter whether I differentiated those without party or ideology from those who called themselves true centrists. Moreover, it had seemed logical to me that political moderates should, to the extent that they were apolitical, have less strong feelings about either liberals or conservatives, and thus report fewer disagreeable encounters. But this was not the case. Although from Figure 2.5 it is not clear which came first, the strong partisanship or the homogeneous social network, one can easily imagine just how mutually reinforcing these two conditions are. Strong partisan views lead one to seek out like-minded partisans, while the homogeneity of the network reinforces those same views.

Cross-Cutting Exposure as Social Capital?

If cross-cutting exposure within social networks cannot be treated as simply a subspecies of political involvement more generally, another possibility is that cross-cutting exposure is a variety of social capital. Indeed, this appears to be what Robert Putnam had in mind when using the phrase "bridging social capital" to differentiate social connections in heterogeneous contexts from "bonding social capital," a term he uses to refer to homogeneous networks.[17]

Although bridging and bonding social capital are typically described as subspecies of a single concept, the conditions likely to promote bonding social capital may be precisely the opposite of those that facilitate bridging social capital. Tight-knit networks of reciprocal obligation are unlikely to go hand in hand with high levels of cross-cutting political conversation. But to the extent that voluntary associations – the most commonly used indicator of social capital – are politically heterogeneous, they may well be indicative of greater cross-cutting exposure. Indeed, Putnam's emphasis on joining voluntary associations rests on the assumption or hope that individuals will eventually make a transition *from* bonding social capital *to* bridging social capital. He cites as examples the kind of voluntary organizations that do not require

[17] Putnam (2000).

shared ideologies or identities, such as groups that form around the arts or sports.

Unfortunately I have found little evidence in support of this thesis in my work, nor in others' work. For one, as shown earlier in Figure 2.2, people apparently do not talk about politics very much in their voluntary associations. Even counting churches and all other forms of voluntary association, social network surveys suggest that at best less than 5 percent of all political discussion dyads know one another through voluntary associations.[18] The number of dyads that involve disagreement is a tiny percentage of that already small number.

Although people report that relatively few political discussion partners have been met through voluntary associations, it is still possible that a person who is typically a joiner of many civic associations will, as an *indirect* result of having a broader network of acquaintances, end up engaging in conversations with those who are not of like mind. To explore this possibility, Figure 2.6 shows the level of cross-cutting exposure among those low, medium, or high in their involvement in voluntary associations. As before, we find the opposite of the relationship hoped for: the extent of bridging as opposed to bonding social capital (at least in the form of talking with those of differing political views) is *negatively* related to the most frequently used indicator of social capital. Those highest in voluntary association memberships are least likely to report cross-cutting political conversations. At least as measured by voluntary association membership, social capital is clearly not the same as cross-cutting exposure.

In theory, voluntary associations are ideal contexts for societal integration.[19] But even if people talked a lot more about politics in their voluntary associations, it is unlikely that this activity would produce much cross-cutting exposure. In practice voluntary associations tend to be "overwhelmingly homogeneous, promoting relations between similar people" and "inhibiting contact between dissimilar ones."[20] The mechanisms through which voluntary associations maintain such high levels of homogeneity include the initial self-selection process, and selective attrition as well. Voluntary associations tend to lose members

---

[18] Mutz & Mondak (2005).

[19] E.g., Blau (1977, 1994).

[20] Popielarz & McPherson (1995, p. 698). See also McPherson & Smith-Lovin (1986, 1987); McPherson, Popielarz, & Drobnic (1992); McPherson & Rotolo (1996).

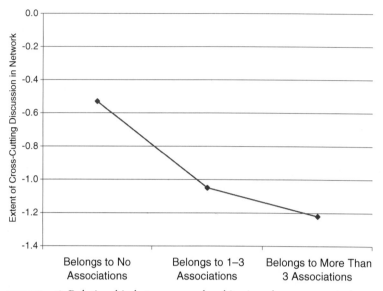

FIGURE 2.6. Relationship between memberships in voluntary associations and extent of cross-cutting discussion in network. (Note: Spencer Foundation Survey, $n = 780$ respondents.)

who are atypical of the group much faster than they lose members in general. When atypical members leave at a higher rate, their doing so ensures ongoing homogeneity. Interaction within voluntary associations does lead to the development of intragroup social trust, but homogeneous associations are less likely to promote *generalized* trust,[21] that is, the kind of trust that crosses lines of difference.

The number of association memberships is clearly not predictive of greater cross-cutting exposure, but some specific kinds of groups may nonetheless expose people to those with oppositional views. The Spencer survey asked respondents directly about the frequency and heterogeneity of political discussion that took place within a voluntary group to which they belonged.[22] Interestingly, of the eighteen possible kinds of voluntary associations in the survey, only two were associated

---

[21] Stolle & Rochon (1998).

[22] Asking respondents this question about all groups of which they are members would have made the survey prohibitively long, as many belonged to a large number of groups. Instead, each respondent was asked about one randomly selected voluntary association of all in which he or she had claimed membership.

with higher than average levels of exposure to political disagreement. Members of school service clubs such as a Parent–Teacher Association had significantly higher levels of cross-cutting exposure, and the same was true of members of professional trade or business organizations. Other group memberships were associated with lower levels of exposure to nonlike-minded views through voluntary associations. For example, members of church or religion-related groups and of political groups both reported significantly less exposure to cross-cutting views through voluntary associations.

On the basis of this overall evidence, it would be difficult to argue that cross-cutting exposure is the same as what is generally termed social capital, at least not as typically measured by voluntary association memberships. This evidence also poses problems for the larger theoretical framework in which voluntary associations are deemed important. The most widely touted benefits of social capital are economic: strong social networks are supposed to reduce "transaction costs" in economic exchange by eliminating the need to monitor others' behavior, and the need to sanction others when they prove less than trustworthy. For these reasons, trust is widely believed to encourage economic growth.[23] These benefits imply the kinds of connections that characterize bridging social capital; that is, connections that extend beyond parochial networks. For example, strong supportive networks *within* disadvantaged communities can do limited good unless they help to connect individuals to wider networks that will enhance their economic and social opportunities.[24] In short, the theoretical benefits attributed to voluntary associations appear to have more to do with *bridging* social capital than with *bonding* social capital, but the operational measures appear to tap homogeneous relations rather than cross-cutting ones.

Is There a Shortage of Cross-Cutting Exposure?

In their 2004 work, Huckfeldt and his colleagues[25] assure us that some exposure to disagreement is the "modal condition" in the United States. But it turns out that this is only the case if a substantial list

[23] Arrow (1972, p. 357).
[24] See Leonard (2004).
[25] See Huckfeldt, Johnson, & Sprague (2004); Huckfeldt, Mendez, & Osborn (2004).

of assumptions are met in a given social environment. Although the model itself is sensible, their empirical observations of the American public do not meet the model's assumptions, nor has empirical work to date generated a confirmatory example. This conclusion also rests on a conceptualization of disagreement that is quite different from what normative theorists have in mind. Theorists suggest that citizens need to be exposed to political views in opposition to their own because this exposure triggers a range of beneficial psychological processes. But to what extent does oppositional exposure actually occur? I examine each of these issues and their implications in turn.

According to Huckfeldt and colleagues:

> If the probability of dyadic agreement within a network is .7, and if the likelihood of agreement is independent across the dyads within a network, then the probability of agreement across all the relationships within a three-discussant network drops to .7³ or .34. In this setting, *disagreement and heterogeneous preferences become the rule rather than the exception within the micro-environments surrounding individual citizens.*[26]

A calculation based on these assumptions suggests that complete and unanimous homogeneity should not be much of a concern. If 66 percent of the population were exposed to at least *some* cross-cutting communication, then one could hardly complain – at least so the argument goes.[27]

Unfortunately not all of these assumptions hold. The .7 probability of agreement within any given dyad is consistent with empirical findings from several network studies. But the assumption of independence in the probabilities of agreement with each successive respondent–discussant in a given network is violated in all surveys of political networks seen to date. For example, in the National Election Studies survey referenced in the article above, the probability of agreement with one's first discussant is significantly positively related to the probability

---

[26] Huckfeldt, Johnson, & Sprague (2004b: p. 68), emphasis in original.

[27] In addition, this optimistic expectation defines homogeneity and heterogeneity in highly unconventional terms. Homogeneity is said to be a problem if and only if there is complete unanimity, and heterogeneity is said to exist if there is a single dissonant view in the network or if any discussant is undecided or has no preference. When a discussant has no known political preference, as is frequently the case, I would suggest that there is no political disagreement to speak of, and thus no exposure to cross-cutting views.

of agreement with the second, and so on and so forth, with each and every pair on down the line to the fourth political discussant.

Another problem with the logic of this framework is even more consequential. It is suggested that the probability of unanimous agreement in a person's network theoretically should be $.7^n$ where n is equal to the total size of the network. Thus, in a three-discussant network, this expectation is .34. The probability that a person is exposed to *any* disagreement at all is thus reasoned to be whatever is left over, that is, 1 minus the probability of unanimous agreement. This produces a very optimistic predicted probability of exposure to cross-cutting views – .66 in this example.

But a quick glance at the empirical data tells us that this theoretical inference is nowhere near the observed probability of experiencing a disagreeable discussant, regardless of the survey analyzed. For example, the NES data that Huckfeldt and colleagues used asks about up to four political discussants, thus producing a $.7^4 = .24$ theoretical probability of unanimous agreement, and a $1 - .24 = .76$ theoretical probability of exposure to some disagreement. The empirical findings in the two studies promoting this rosy expectation do not provide bottom-line figures for the percentage of the public that is exposed to disagreement. But on the basis of my calculations using these same data, the *actual* probability of being exposed to *at least one disagreeable discussant* in the NES study is .34. Why the huge discrepancy between .76 in theory and .34 in practice?

In part it occurs because most people cannot list as many as four people with whom they discuss politics, thus the theoretical expectation for network size – that all respondents will have four discussants – is overly optimistic. In reality only 20 percent of the NES sample met this assumption, even though this is a necessary condition for the theoretical calculation to approximate real-world findings. So reality falls far short of this promising prediction.

Important differences in conceptual definitions of disagreement also come into play in these differing conclusions. Huckfeldt and his colleagues define disagreement in terms of *lack of agreement*, as noted in the preceding calculations. This means that if a respondent's discussant did not support any candidate whatsoever, he or she was still counted as contributing disagreement to the person's network. Apolitical or undecided discussants thus contributed heavily toward the conclusion that "disagreement is the modal condition among citizens – most citizens experience disagreement and divergent political preferences within these networks."[28] Indeed, in the NES sample, counting those without candidate preferences as disagreeable discussants makes that figure nearly 60 percent, compared to just over 30 percent if one counts only those who have oppositional preferences.

Beyond the conceptual mismatch, respondents who did not have any political discussants at all were discarded from Huckfeldt's calculations, even though these people obviously lack exposure to disagreement as well. This analytic decision makes the observed incidence of cross-cutting exposure appear higher. If the probability of being exposed to any disagreement is adjusted so that the sample incorporates those voters who do not have political discussants, then the probability of encountering political disagreement drops still further from .34 to an even lower .27.

Because some measures of disagreement such as the NES ones are based exclusively on presidential vote choice, the samples are further limited to only those who report having voted for president. If we include in the NES sample nonvoters who nonetheless expressed a preference for one candidate or the other, then the percentage of the public exposed to disagreement drops to 23 percent.

There is a big difference between a country in which 76 percent of people are exposed to some oppositional political views (the theoretical prediction based on four discussants) and one in which only 23 percent are so exposed (the observation based on asking people about four discussants). The precise numbers in any given study are less important than the overall very limited extent to which cross-cutting exposure occurs. Although all operational definitions are necessarily somewhat arbitrary, exposure to an apolitical or nonopinionated discussant does not seem at all what theorists have in mind when they speak of the virtues of exposure to disagreement.

This discrepancy brings into sharp relief the need for closer connections between theory and empirical work. Which concept is more consistent with what political theory suggests is of benefit to individuals in a democratic system? For purposes of the kinds of benefits explored in this book, it seems essential that citizens be exposed to more than

---

[28] Huckfeldt, Johnson, & Sprague (2004, p. 19).

simply discussants who express no opinions. What is central to triggering the social psychological benefits of disagreement is that people confront others who have political views in opposition to theirs. It is this event that sets into motion the processes envisioned by political theorists.

In the NES example, as in many others, under one-quarter of the U.S. population reported exposure to even one person of oppositional political views through their personal networks. That low a level of exposure seems to me a genuine cause for concern. To the extent that reinforcement overwhelmingly dominates genuine questioning of the merits of one's views, the benefits of cross-cutting exposure are far less likely.

Are Bigger Networks Better?

The logic behind the model described in the previous section naturally leads to the conclusion that the "level of political homogeneity within networks declines rapidly as a function of increased network size."[29] Thus a casual reader might assume that people who have larger networks have less homogeneous networks as a result. Is the solution to the problem of hearing too many echoes of one's own voice simply to promote larger political networks?

This prescriptive solution is questionable. It is widely believed that bigger political discussion networks will naturally lead to greater exposure to cross-cutting views and all of the benefits this might confer. After all, the theoretical model described earlier predicts that a four-person network has a greater probability of exposure to disagreement ($1 - .7^4 = 76$) than a three-person network ($1 - .7^3 = 66$).

So long as people are encouraged to have bigger networks, the promise of cross-cutting exposure will be fulfilled, at least so the argument goes. As shown by the solid black area in Figure 2.7, in a literal sense this assertion is absolutely correct: the solid black area indicating the average number of discussants holding oppositional political views clearly climbs with increasing network size, from .19 to .85. This increase of .66 indicates a significantly greater expected number of oppositional discussants if one's network is large.

---

[29] Huckfeldt, Mendez, & Osborn (2004, p. 72).

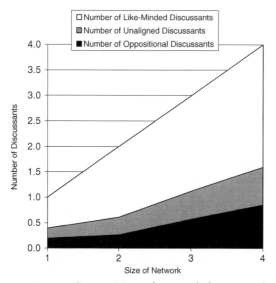

FIGURE 2.7. Composition of network by network size. (Note: Data from National Election Studies 2000.)

But what this analysis misses is what is shown by the other two areas in Figure 2.7. The number of *like-minded* discussants increases with network size to an even greater degree, from .61 to 2.41, that is, by 1.80. Thus in a larger network, the number of discussants who agree swamps the oppositional voices to an even greater degree than in much smaller networks.

In parallel areas of study where homogeneity is a concern – such as the racial composition of schools or neighborhoods – homogeneity in a social context is still considered problematic and influential even when it is not absolute. The presence of one minority family living in an otherwise entirely white neighborhood would not lead to the conclusion that lack of racial diversity is no longer a problem in this area. One can obviously take such analogies too far, but in theories of deliberative communication, it is likewise questionable whether just one oppositional voice in a sea of reinforcement is ideal for producing the kinds of benefits that cross-cutting exposure promises.

The number of oppositional and politically unaligned discussants in the network does go up slightly as the size of the network increases. But as illustrated in Figure 2.8, no matter how you construct an indicator of

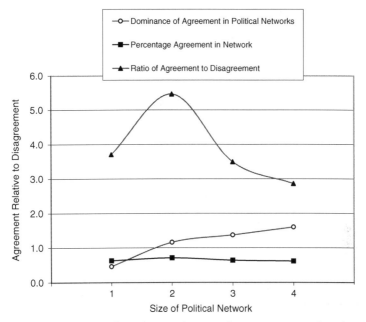

FIGURE 2.8. Extent of agreement relative to disagreement in political networks, by size of network. (Note: Data from the National Election Studies 2000. Entries represent [1] dominance: the total number of same presidential choice respondents minus oppositional discussants; [2] percentage: the number of like-minded discussants of the total number in the network; and [3] ratio: the number of agreeable discussants divided by the number of disagreeable discussants.)

heterogeneity in the network, it is difficult to argue that larger networks alleviate the homogeneity problem. The solid line marked by squares in Figure 2.8 shows the average percentage of people in a network who can be expected to reinforce the main respondent's views, by network size. The flat line shows no evidence of declining homogeneity as network size increases. The line marked by circles illustrates the number of agreeable discussants minus the number of disagreeable discussants by network size. By this indicator, agreement dominates disagreement to an even *greater* extent among those with large networks. Finally, the line marked by triangles in Figure 2.8 illustrates the ratio of agreeable to disagreeable discussants, again by network size. Here the extent of agreement climbs steeply from one- to two-discussant networks, the opposite of the model prediction, then declines back to initial levels with networks of size three, and further toward heterogeneity at size four. And even at its most heterogeneous, the ratio of agreement to disagreement remains extremely high, at 3:1 at the largest network size.

These patterns provide little reassurance that large network size alleviates the dominance of reinforcement over cross-cutting exposure. Even the indicator most supportive of this thesis – the ratio of agreement to disagreement – presents a more complex pattern than declining agreement with increasing network size. Larger networks alone do not guarantee adequate levels of cross-cutting exposure.

Where Does Cross-Cutting Exposure Originate?

The descriptive account of cross-cutting exposure that I have provided thus far makes it clear that exposure to oppositional views should not be treated as simply another form of political participation that can be subsumed under this widely researched concept. Nor should it be considered a form of social capital, at least not according to standard conceptualizations or operationalizations. Moreover, it does not seem to correspond with any of the usual suspects in predictable ways.

This naturally leads to the question of where cross-cutting exposure comes from. Why are some people exposed to a relatively greater extent of oppositional political views in their networks than others? The conventional answer to this question is that it is a function of two factors: individual choice and environmental constraint. Individuals may select friends and associates who are of like mind politically, and this appears to be particularly likely when politics is of great importance to a person. Selective exposure is likely to account for the fact that the networks of highly partisan and politically active people are more dominated by like-minded discussants. Politics is important to their lives and identities, thus their friends are likely to be chosen at least in part on the basis of this dimension of similarity. People who deem politics a relatively minor aspect of their lives and identities are less likely to take this dimension of similarity into account.

A second factor useful in explaining who talks to whom is environmental constraint. Environmental constraint suggests that people's interactions with others are, to some extent, circumscribed by their

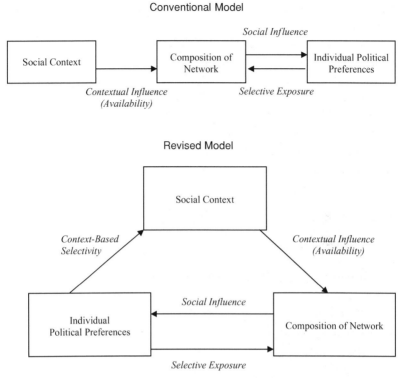

FIGURE 2.9. Conventional and revised models of relationships among social context, political networks, and individual political preferences.

social environments, which supply them with more people of some kinds of political views than of others. Regardless of their own views and motivations, they interact more with the kinds of people who surround them, whatever their politics might be.

As illustrated at the top of Figure 2.9, to the extent that selectivity is exercised by individuals, one generally expects the heterogeneity of their personal networks to decrease. Although there are surely some exceptions, we know on the basis of numerous network studies that the overwhelming tendency is toward like-minded interpersonal contact. In contrast, what has been dubbed "environmental," "structural," or "contextual" influence is assumed to be the involuntary element of social life, and thus increases the potential for exposure to difference. Environments are traditionally understood as external, exogenous factors that impose constraints on people's ability to exercise selectivity:

"Contexts are structurally imposed, whereas networks are individually constructed."[30]

Personal networks are widely acknowledged to be individually constructed and subject to partisan selectivity, as shown by the reverse arrow in Figure 2.9, but social contexts are not.[31] On the basis of these assumptions, individuals and their selective patterns of association are essentially the enemies of cross-cutting discourse. Environmental–contextual influences are the protagonists because they are assumed to be outside an individual's personal control and thus facilitate involuntary social interactions.[32]

De Facto Selective Exposure

The troubling aspect of the conventional model is that it does not take into account the burgeoning evidence suggesting that people choose their social contexts based on lifestyle considerations that are related to political views. An individual's ability to control his or her social interactions is undoubtedly constrained by the social contexts he or she inhabits. But in the contemporary United States, the emerging consensus is that people's residential contexts are hardly exogenous.

Demographic trends suggest that people are increasingly choosing a place of residence on the basis of factors that lead to greater segregation from those different from them. Residential patterns have moved toward increasingly spatially segregated living on the basis of race,[33] education, age,[34] and income.[35] In part, this is because advances in communication and transportation have made place of residence more of a consumer lifestyle choice that can be separated from the location of employment. To the extent that this census-based evidence translates to similarities in political attitudes, communication across

---

[30] Huckfeldt & Sprague (1995a), emphasis in original.

[31] Ibid., p. 16. In studies of the persuasive effects of social contexts, this is an extremely useful methodological assumption, because it allows one to draw causal inferences from cross-sectional data. When the composition of people's networks affects their preferences, it is assumed to do so by means of one or more of several processes of social influence.

[32] Ibid., p. 11.

[33] Harrison & Bennett (1995); Massey & Denton (1993).

[34] Frey (1995).

[35] Levy (1995).

lines of difference should be increasingly unlikely, at least in residential settings.[36] Thus the traditional dichotomy between externally imposed social contexts and individually constructed personal networks may be breaking down as one's environment becomes increasingly a matter of individual choice.

The balkanization that has been documented thus far does not suggest that hordes of Americans are purposely choosing to live among people who share their political views. Indeed, few Americans assign politics such a central role in their lives. De facto selectivity is far more likely,[37] that is, people may choose a particular location because it is convenient to local co-ops, or a golf course, or the schools they want their children to attend, and they find themselves among others who based their selection on similar considerations. The initial goal may not have been politically like-minded neighbors, but that is achieved to the extent that lifestyle considerations correlate with political perspectives. Instead, people are likely to choose environments because they are populated by "people like me" in the sense of shared lifestyles, values, or even market position.[38]

Interestingly, scholars have assumed that political interactions occur purely as by-products of other interactions, with no consideration as to topic.[39] The assumptions to date have been that (1) social contexts are externally imposed and exogenous influences on political networks and (2) selectivity in the choice of individual discussion partners is largely apolitical.[40] As suggested by the bottom panel of Figure 2.9, these assumptions probably require revision. Selective exposure based on political agreement or on factors closely correlated with political

---

[36] Calhoun (1988).

[37] See Freedman & Sears (1965) for details on this distinction.

[38] E.g., Turow (1997).

[39] E.g., Brown (1981); McPhee, Smith, & Ferguson (1963).

[40] Putnam (1966), for example, found that partisanship was not a major factor in friendship formation. Huckfeldt & Sprague (1995a) suggest that people choose friends primarily for reasons other than politics and then have incidental political discussions. In other words, it is purely a by-product of other interactions. However, the network a respondent mentions when asked about discussing politics is not the same as that mentioned for other topics. For example, we know there are important differences between networks that people mention for the discussion of "important problems" and those involved in discussions of politics; see Huckfeldt & Sprague (1995b). In addition, Huckfeldt & Sprague (1995a) found that when the discussion partner disagreed with the main respondent's views, the respondent was more likely to avoid political discussion with that person.

agreement must play a significant role in influencing the kinds of political interactions that people have and the kind of political networks they form. There is simply no other way to account for the extremely high levels of homogeneity routinely found in research on political networks. As John Hlinko, founder of ActForLove.org, an Internet dating site for liberals, put it, "Politics is a proxy for your basic values. This is what people care about. If you don't share the same core values as someone, it's going to be really tough for (a relationship) to take off."[41] Similar Web sites, such as Conservativematch.com, SingleRepublicans.com, and LiberalHearts.com, also suggest that although looking for love may be a nonpartisan endeavor, for some politics serves as a useful shorthand.

The bottom panel of Figure 2.9 provides a revised account of the likely relationships between people's social contexts, their networks, and their political views, one that assumes that political preferences can affect choice of context as well as choice of discussants. Selection effects can operate at either level. To the extent that contexts are chosen rather than imposed, they reflect the same processes of selectivity used in the choice of friends and associates.

Because political homogeneity and social homogeneity are linked, demographic trends have potentially important consequences for the political homogeneity of social contexts. How large the consequences are remains to be seen. But the explosion of so-called gated communities, retirement communities, and so forth, reflects further efforts to live among those with similar interests and concerns. Residential communities are increasingly "enclaves of people who have made similar life-style choices. These life-style enclaves – especially suburban and exurban ones – are characterized by an extraordinary homophilia."[42] As cities expanded, they became more like a cluster of suburbs each with its own convenient commercial area, its own recreational space, and so forth. These types of communities, typically located on the fringes of central cities, are thriving in the United States.[43]

[41] Article by Lisa Baertlein, "Livewire: Web Aids Search for the Right – or Left – Mate." Reuters, September 8, 2004.
[42] Calhoun (1988, p. 226).
[43] Gated communities represent an even more extreme form of maintaining homogeneity and separation. See Blakely & Snyder (1997).

Is America Exceptional?

The revised model in Figure 2.9 suggests that multiple social forces are pushing in the direction of greater homogeneity. It is easy to find fault with overall levels of cross-cutting political discourse in the United States. But is America truly qualitatively different from other countries in the degree to which its citizens seek to avoid political conversations that involve oppositional views? This common view, also voiced by the person writing to Miss Manners's column, is widely believed, though to my knowledge without empirical verification.

Cross-national data on this dimension of social experience are in short supply, but two crude comparisons are possible. First, the World Values Surveys[44] include one general question asking respondents about their frequency of political discussion with others. Based on this item, which was asked in eighty-one different countries, the United States ranks in the 60th percentile for highest frequency of political discussion, behind Israel (100th percentile), Poland (75th), Sweden and Greece (83rd), Norway (95th), and the Netherlands (70th), to provide just a few examples. But Americans are also far *more* engaged in political discussion than people in Great Britain (6th percentile), Singapore (10th), Canada (36th), and most Latin American countries. Despite many pleas for "reinvigorating" public discussion in the United States, it appears that Americans are relatively talkative compared to citizens of many other countries.

Unfortunately, these comparisons tell us little about the extent to which Americans engage in *cross-cutting* discussions relative to other countries. For these purposes, I drew on a twelve-country comparison made possible by the CNEP surveys. If selective exposure is taking place to a greater extent in the United States than elsewhere (whether for structural or individually motivated reasons), then one would expect to see higher levels of homogeneity in the political discussion networks of Americans relative to those of citizens of other countries.

Quantifying the homogeneity of networks cross-nationally is a complex, though not insurmountable task. To do so I sacrificed detail in the measures in order to ensure the comparability of indicators

---

[44] See Inglehart et al. (2004) for information from the World Values Survey.

across countries.[45] Rough comparisons can be made by evaluating the percentage of respondents who do or do not have particular numbers of political discussants with whom they talk politics. Spouses were eliminated from the pool of discussants because some countries directly asked about spouses before the general discussant battery, and others did not. Because it is discussion outside the immediate family that is most central to public discussion, this seemed a reasonable way to create comparable measures across respondents of all nationalities.

Consistently with the World Values data, the CNEP surveys confirmed that Americans are among the more talkative populations when it comes to political matters. But more importantly, these network surveys allowed a comparative sense of the extent of disagreement in Americans' political discussion networks.[46] In order to ensure that the results of this comparison were more than simply an artifact of different numbers of parties in different countries, I used a combination of several survey items to determine whether the party the respondent favored was similar to or different from the party advocated by the discussants. In other words, the fact that a respondent and his or her discussant favored different parties was not considered sufficient evidence of disagreement in a dyad. If disagreement were defined as simply supporting different parties, then countries with partisans split among many smaller parties would probabilistically register less agreement and more disagreement. After all, random chance alone would predict that a discussant who supported a relatively small party would encounter more partisans from other parties, even if all social interactions were completely random. Using that measurement scheme, more parties would mean more disagreement by chance alone.

To circumvent these problems, I used respondents' perceptions of the proximity of their discussant's party to their own interests in order to assess whether or not a given party was similar to or different from the respondent's own political interests. By combining the party proximity

---

[45] For example, although there are scales for frequency of political talk for dyads in the CNEP surveys, the scales are too vague in terminology and too irregular across countries and languages to facilitate reliable comparisons.

[46] To make this comparison across countries, some that asked first about spouses and others that did not, I compared the like-mindedness of the first and second nonspouse discussants, since these were available for all of these countries.

measures with information on which party was supported by each of the respondent's discussants, it was possible to ascertain whether the dyad was roughly in agreement or in disagreement. Thus in a country with many political parties, two people of differing party loyalties might nonetheless be deemed in agreement because the respondent perceived both parties as at least somewhat representative of his or her interests. Likewise, a nonpartisan could still be in agreement with his or her discussant if the respondent perceived the discussant's party to be favorable to his or her own interests.[47]

In Figure 2.10, the vertical axes in both the upper and lower panels represent the extent to which partisanship among discussants is either similar to (high) or dissimilar to (low) that of the respondent. It was calculated by taking the percentage of each sample in which the partisanship of the discussant was in the same direction as that of the main respondent, minus the percentage in opposition to the main respondent. Thus high scores on the y axis indicate greater net agreement. The top panel shows these figures for the first nonspouse discussant who was named, and the lower panel shows the same for the second discussant mentioned. On the y axis, o represents the case in which equal percentages of respondents see their discussants as favoring their own views and favoring oppositional views; positive scores indicate that a greater number of respondents perceive their discussants to favor their own views. Dyads that are apolitical or neither in agreement or disagreement have no net effect on this percentage.

Solely on the basis of the vertical location of the point labeled USA, we see that Americans social relationships are indeed exceptional when it comes to the extent to which respondents and discussants hold similar political perspectives. Of all countries studied, the United States shows the highest degree of political similarity between respondents and their discussants. For both the first and second named discussants, the United States is highest in the extent to which discussants hold political views that are, on balance, similar to the respondents' own views. Thus Americans' political networks are also the most lacking in political confrontation.

---

[47] For several countries, respondents were asked about what party or candidate the discussant supported, but the technique for determining agreeable and disagreeable dyads was parallel.

First Nonspouse Discussant Named

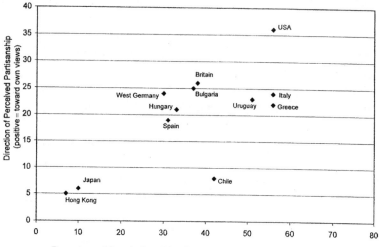

Percentage of Sample Perceiving Partisanship in First Nonspouse Discussant

Second Nonspouse Discussant Named

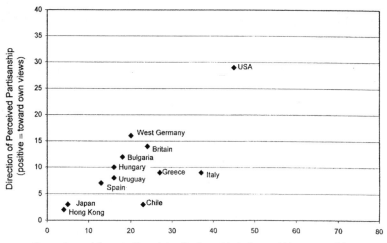

Percentage of Sample Perceiving Partisanship in Second Nonspouse Discussant

FIGURE 2.10. Relationship between extent of partisanship of discussants and direction of partisanship relative to respondent.

The location of countries across the horizontal axis in Figure 2.10 indicates the total percentage of discussants in each country perceived to be partisan in some fashion or another, regardless of direction; that is, they favor some party or candidate, regardless of which one. In a sense, the x axis serves as a measure of the degree of politicization of that country's population; places where virtually everyone has partisan views will naturally fall farther out on the x axis, with countries with fewer identifiable partisans closer to zero. According to this indicator, the United States is similar to Italy and Greece on the basis of the top panel of Figure 2.10. In all three countries just under 60 percent of respondents report a partisan first discussant, that is, one who is known to favor a candidate or party.

I have plotted the extent of agreement between respondents and discussants on the same graph as the overall extent of partisanship in the population in order to illustrate a simple, but nonetheless important point. Higher overall levels of partisanship coincide with populations that, on the whole, have more agreeable political conversations.[48] What the pattern in these figures suggests is that the more politicized the country is, the more selective exposure comes into play, though it is impossible to say whether it is of the motivated or de facto variety. To the extent that political preferences are salient and well known, selective approach and avoidance are that much easier. High levels of partisanship – whether it is favoritism for parties or for particular candidates – make it easier to select congenial discussion partners. Moreover, the highly simplified two-party system in the United States may make these distinctions more visible than in countries that have many parties.

Highly partisan political environments pose a paradox: on the one hand, the existence of large numbers of people who hold readily identifiable political preferences would tend to suggest a vibrant, active political culture. On the other hand, it appears that many citizens in such an environment will isolate themselves among those of largely like-minded views, thus making it difficult for cross-cutting political discourse to transpire.

Based on the comparative evidence in Figure 2.10, the problem in the United States is not that people do not talk about politics enough; it

[48] $r = .72, p < .01.$

is that when people do talk about politics, they are particularly likely
to talk with those of like mind. Such interactions will tend to have
more to do with rooting for the same candidate or political cause than
with exploring political options or discussing differences of opinion. In
short, these interactions do little to promote the cause of deliberation
among members of the general public.

Answered and Unanswered Questions

Having one's views challenged has probably never been the norm in the
United States when discussing politics in informal settings. As Converse
noted back in 1964:

> A member of that tiny elite that comments publicly about political currents
> (probably some fraction of 1% of a population) spends most of his time in
> informal communication about politics with others in the same select group. He
> rarely encounters a conversation in which his assumptions of shared contextual
> grasp of political ideas are challenged.[49]

Nowadays, more than the "tiny elite" described by Converse appear to
comment on political affairs – at least in informal conversations with
their friends and acquaintances. But his observation about the highly
parochial nature of those conversations remains as true as ever. Insofar
as cross-cutting exposure is deemed highly desirable by contemporary
social scientists, this condition is lamentable. The solution resides in
part in more political conversations among "weak ties," that is those
who are not intimate friends or family members.

  For this reason, it is not entirely clear that social theorists have the
correct prescription for the American condition. Contemporary social
science is full of romanticized allusions to a better, more cozy and comfortable America of the past. Unfortunately, the place "where everybody knows your name," is probably also the place where everybody
feels roughly the same as you do about politics. I am, of course, over-
stating this relationship to make a point. But the descriptive patterns
in this chapter illuminate potentially negative aspects of living in environments characterized by dense, close-knit social networks. Although
such communities have many positive characteristics to recommend

---

[49] Converse (1964).

them, most of these benefits are the same as those of the small towns once lionized by mass society theory. Communities of dense networks may be more like the warm and fuzzy small towns of yesteryear, but they can be exclusionary and homogeneous as well. They are not the locales where cross-cutting exposure and deliberative democracy would flourish.

To the extent that we consider cross-cutting conversation essential to democracy, we must look to more casual associations rather than dense networks of reciprocal obligation. Despite the many virtues of deliberation that have been claimed, few claim that conversations across lines of difference are comfortable or particularly enjoyable.[50] Indeed, often what people mean when they say they "feel part of a community" is that there are many other people just like them living in their communities, people who share their values and lifestyles to a significant degree.

Although people may prefer friends and acquaintances who are in political agreement with them, many are, nonetheless, exposed to those with views unlike their own on a fairly regular basis. They hear the other side, not so often by choice as *in spite of* the choices they make. The workplace appears to be the social context in which political conversation across lines of difference most often takes place. In fact, the workplace makes more widely studied social contexts such as the neighborhood and voluntary associations pale in comparison. These contexts have serious shortcomings as public spaces for fostering cross-cutting discourse, including the amount of political dialogue that tends to transpire in groups and in the neighborhood, and the extent to which the little political dialogue that does take place tends to be characterized by agreement.

This chapter also demonstrates that political networks in the United States are not already so diverse that we can abandon concerns about them. Instead, the prospects for diversity in Americans' interpersonal

[50] An exception to this claim can be found in James Fishkin's deliberative poll weekends, in which random samples of citizens from across the country are brought together in a hotel for the weekend to talk about political issues, to listen to and question political elites, and so forth, with all expenses paid. Many participants in deliberative polls say they enjoyed the experience. It is unclear if it would be as enjoyable if it took place in an unstructured, unmoderated environment at home or with people they knew and would continue to see on an ongoing basis.

environments may have become increasingly bleak in the last few decades, with greater emphasis on individual control over choice of social context, as well as over choice of individual discussants. On a more optimistic note, the over-time trends documented thus far have been strictly for residential contexts, so they do not necessarily indicate greater agreement in people's political networks overall.

Likewise, it is not safe for social scientists to assume that the many social contexts people inhabit as part of their day to day lives – all potential contexts for conversations across lines of difference – are immune to selection processes. Evidence as to whether the mass public is sorting into more homogeneous areas is mixed and heavily debated.[51] But what is far less controversial is that Americans' social environments and exercise of choice provide tremendous *potential* for segregation and polarization.

Finally, to answer the question posed at the beginning of this chapter, the extent to which people's networks include conversations across lines of political difference is clearly not a surrogate for some already well-studied concept. The extent of exposure to cross-cutting political views in a person's network cannot be treated as a subspecies of political participation, nor of social capital. The heterogeneity of a person's network is not even a positive function of his or her amount of political conversation more generally. The implications of these patterns – both beneficial and deleterious ones – form the substance of Chapters 3 and 4.

---

[51] For an overview of competing claims, see the final report from the Princeton University conference, "The Polarization of American Politics: Myth or Reality?" December 2004. http://www.princeton.edu/~csdp/events/pdfs/Polarizationfinal.pdf.

3

Benefits of Hearing the Other Side

Theorists extol the virtues of political talk, foundations spend millions of dollars to encourage people of opposing views to talk to one another, and civic journalism advocates plan special meetings to foster more political conversations across lines of difference. Yet what do we really know about beneficial outcomes of political talk as it occurs in day to day life? More to the point, do we have convincing evidence that hearing the other side improves individuals or societies in some tangible way?

For the most part, arguments for the centrality of political discussion among ordinary Americans have been highly theoretical in nature. This is true in two senses. Not only are these expectations derived from various brands of political theory as outlined in Chapter 1, but with few exceptions they remain entirely hypothetical expectations. The same is true with respect to the benefits of hearing the other side, a subset of the many claims about the benefits of political talk.

As deliberation and deliberative democracy have become buzzwords for what democracy needs, scholars have become increasingly interested in documenting and harnessing this supposedly beneficial force. A spate of recent studies has attempted to manipulate deliberation by bringing people together to talk in small groups.[1] These studies

---

[1] See Morrell (2000); Muhlberger & Butts (1998); Price & Cappella (2001); Simon & Sulkin (2000); Weber (1998).

have provided many new insights on what happens when people are compelled to talk to one another about controversial issues, but the broad and variable nature of their interactions has made it difficult to determine which aspects of the experience are producing the observed effects. Deliberation is a conglomeration of many variables, and disentangling their effects when they are varied simultaneously is often impossible.

Some of the earliest and best-known examples of empirical research on deliberation are from Fishkin's specially organized deliberative forums. "Deliberative polling," a registered trademark for Fishkin's particular version of a national town meeting, involves a random sample of citizens who are initially interviewed by telephone about the public policy issues that will form the theme of the deliberative poll. Respondents are then invited to gather somewhere in the country for a weekend in order to discuss the issues, with all expenses paid by the organizers. Participants who agree are sent briefing materials on the topic of the deliberative poll in advance. The weekend gathering then gives participants opportunities to talk to experts and to political leaders, as well as to one another. At the end of the weekend, participants are surveyed again.[2]

Deliberative forums have the advantage of allowing pretest and posttest measures of likely effects, and of providing an unusual degree of control over the types of interactions in which citizens engage. Researchers know precisely who talks to whom and what they both say. So far so good from the perspective of a strong research design. Unfortunately, even studies of deliberative polls have significant shortcomings as tests of deliberative theory. To be fair, many of these problems are not unique to studies of deliberative events. The well-worn axiom that all research designs are flawed in some respect is as valid here as in any other area. But what is especially troubling about tests based on deliberative polls is that they are often lacking both in the strength of causal inferences that may be drawn from them (i.e., internal validity) *and* in the extent to which they can be generalized to deliberation as it occurs naturally (i.e., external validity). Given the tremendous effort and expense that such events require, one would hope that they

---

[2] Fishkin (1991).

could provide good leverage on at least one of these two important dimensions.[3]

One difficulty with drawing causal inferences about the power of deliberation from deliberative polling is that several independent variables are manipulated at the same time. Those who agree to participate are sent briefing materials in advance, for example. They are exposed to still more information from experts and politicians at the event itself. Ultimately, one cannot determine whether the benefits that accrue are due to information passed on by the political elites, informational materials distributed by organizers in advance of the events themselves, and/or the deliberation that takes place among participants during the weekend. In essence, "deliberation" has been redefined as an entire package of interventions, some of which are part and parcel of deliberative theory and others of which are not.

One well might ask, "Who cares whether the manipulations are confounded, so long as they work?" But knowing which element or elements in this package of treatments has an impact results in strikingly different interpretations. For example, if the educational materials that are mailed out are responsible for desirable effects, then what we have is an argument in favor of public information campaigns. On the other hand, if the presence of political experts and issue elites at the deliberative sessions is what drives the desirable outcomes, then we have an argument for a more top-down view of how democracy might operate most beneficially. Finally, if positive outcomes are a function of participants' talking to others of equal status in a civil setting, then we would have evidence in support of deliberation as a means to enrich citizens. Unfortunately, it is unclear from research to date whether results are due to the educational efforts associated with the polls, the direct personal attention political elites give to ordinary Americans during these events, the deliberation among citizens, the extent of crosscutting conversation in those deliberations, or some other aspect of the forums.

Potential confounding is problematic for the interpretation of findings, and the design of deliberative polls exacerbates the problem.

---

[3] For a recent example of a study of the effects of deliberation on opinions, see Barabas (2004).

Participants are interviewed before the deliberative weekend, as well as after it, and any change that occurs from one time to the next is attributed to deliberation. Even if one is willing to treat the entire package of activities associated with these events as "deliberation," a one-group pretest–posttest design does not easily permit causal claims.[4] Without a control group of some kind who did not deliberate, it is easy to see how such changes might come about with or without deliberation. Consider deliberative polling that takes place before an election. With or without such an event, one would expect political interest at time 2 to be higher than at time 1, if only because the election is closer at hand.

Some studies of deliberative events have constructed "control groups" after the fact, using those who refused to participate in the deliberative weekend, or concurrent random samples of the population. But self-selection and the resulting noncomparable groups make this solution less desirable. Unfortunately, the real solution – a study in which those who are willing to participate are randomly assigned to attend or not – has yet to be done. Some recent work comes much closer to this goal,[5] but we have yet to disentangle the effects of informational materials, expert advice, and deliberation itself successfully.

Deliberative polls also face problems of external validity. Even if the beneficial effects could safely be attributed to a deliberative weekend, what would that say about deliberation as it happens in the naturally occurring world? How similar is this experience to the one people might have in day to day life? Americans report that they are very unlikely to talk about politics at public meetings.[6] But those who accept an invitation to a deliberative poll are obliged to do so. Although they are, nonetheless, a demographically representative sample, the generalizability of findings from specially orchestrated forums to everyday political life is an open question. As noted, the presence of briefing materials, expert panels, group moderators, and the like, "make the formal on-site deliberations very different from naturally occurring discussion in the real world."[7] Unless a significant proportion of the American

---

[4] Cook & Campbell (1979, p. 99).
[5] See Farrar, Fishkin, Green, List, Luskin, & Paluck (2003).
[6] Conover & Searing (1998). See also Mansbridge (1983).
[7] Farrar et al. (2003, p. 4).

population participated in a deliberative event for each political choice they were asked to make, we would not expect deliberative polling, or deliberative meetings more generally, to have a large impact on the quality of mass opinion. The expense of such an undertaking would be well beyond the realm of the practical. Moreover, by some definitions participation of this kind would not count as deliberation, which is supposed to be something citizens do for and among themselves, rather than something elites induce them to do.

Beyond deliberative forums and deliberative polls, still other strategies have been used to gauge the impact of political conversation in other settings, particularly in dyads or small groups. In an extensive review of this literature, Mendelberg sounds a note of caution about expecting consistently positive outcomes from deliberation.[8] Instead, her overview suggests that beneficial effects are highly contingent. Attempts to deliberate can sometimes be helpful, and sometimes not, depending upon a host of other factors. These findings are also mixed and inconclusive because of differences in what one "counts" as deliberation, and in what kinds of outcomes are deemed beneficial. Opinion change, for example, is often cited as evidence that deliberation "works," but it is unclear under what conditions one should deem this change beneficial versus harmful.

In order to understand which aspects of the deliberation "package" are important, they need to be unpacked into smaller, more specifiable components. This appears to be the only strategy with the potential to make sense of these inconsistent findings. And although it would be naive to expect scholars to reach agreement on a single definition of the necessary and sufficient conditions for deliberation, I think it is realistic to expect that scholars may come to understand the beneficial roles played by different elements of political and social interaction. For these reasons, in examining potential beneficial effects, I focus strictly on one dimension of deliberative experience – the extent to which political conversations expose people to "the other side." Overall, this chapter suggests that despite the disappointing frequency of cross-cutting conversations illustrated in Chapter 2, hearing the other side does – even in its highly imperfect manifestations – have some beneficial consequences for citizens of a democracy.

---

[8] Mendelberg (2002).

Exposure to diverse political views is obviously tied to a wide range of outcomes that are valued in democratic systems. But it would be an overly simplistic reading of deliberative theory to suggest that it assumes only good can flow from cross-cutting interactions; conversations among those of differing views also have been acknowledged to hold the capacity to promote bitter arguments, violence, and/or a hostile silence.[9] A level of civility or politeness in conversations across lines of political difference is assumed to be essential to its assumed benefits.[10] As Kingwell points out, in order to obtain benefits and sustain relationships that make cross-cutting discourse possible, discussants must at times refrain from saying all they could say in the interest of smooth social interaction. This type of civility via "not-saying . . . contributes to smooth social interaction, makes for tolerance of diversity and conditions a regard for the claims and interests of others."[11] So although exposure to differing views holds the *potential* for tremendous benefits, to realize these benefits, exposure must occur in a context where the collective project of getting along with one another in society is primary, and the elucidation of differences secondary.

The Social Psychological Plausibility of Beneficial Consequences

There are obviously dozens of empirically testable hypotheses embedded in the assertions of deliberative theory. Unfortunately existing survey data provide few opportunities to test them. As discussed in Chapter 2, the kinds of items needed to study political talk and exposure to disagreement in particular are included in several network surveys, but measures of the outcomes that theoretically ought to be related to them are typically absent. Most social network studies are designed to evaluate attitude change due to pressures within social networks. Will people feel compelled to vote the way their friends and neighbors do, for example? The formation of political opinions – the focus of the earliest political network studies – tends to remain the focus today. And as a result we lack the evidence needed to evaluate most of these ideas.

---

[9] Scorza (1998).
[10] Kingwell (1995).
[11] Kingwell (1995, p. 219).

For these reasons, I commissioned an original national survey to include indicators of people's exposure to politically like-minded and differently minded people, *and* the kinds of beneficial outcomes this contact is assumed to engender – an awareness of oppositional perspectives, a deeper understanding of reasons behind one's own views, and support for the civil liberties of groups whose politics one dislikes. Funded by the Spencer Foundation, this survey made it possible to examine three independent beneficial effects of cross-cutting networks. Communication environments that expose people to non–like-minded political views were hypothesized to promote (1) greater awareness of rationales for one's own viewpoints, (2) greater awareness of rationales for oppositional viewpoints, and (3) greater tolerance.

How plausible are such benefits from the perspective of what is known about the social psychology of human interaction? The first benefit rests on the assumption that confronting differences prompts people to reflect on the reasons for their own beliefs. This process is assumed to occur either in preparation for defending one's own positions or as a result of an internal need to rationalize or explain why one's own views differ from others'. Studies of cognitive response generally support the plausibility of such a reaction; exposure to counterattitudinal advocacy enhances the production of counterarguments, particularly for highly involving topics.[12] Consistent with this argument, Green, Visser, and Tetlock found that people became more aware of and able to balance valid arguments on both sides of an issue when they were exposed to strong arguments on both sides of an issue *and* anticipated having to justify their views to opinionated representatives of the conflicting sides, an experimental condition simulating a cross-cutting personal network.[13]

The second proposed benefit, that cross-cutting exposure promotes greater awareness of oppositional viewpoints, simply assumes that exposure to dissimilar views imparts new information. Psychologically this effect demands nothing more than a straightforward learning process whereby rationales are transmitted from one person to another. The greatest limitation on its plausibility is the infrequency with which

---

[12] Petty & Cacioppo (1979). Mutz (1998) also demonstrates this process directly in the context of political issue positions.

[13] Green, Visser, & Tetlock (2000).

political conversations are likely to reach the level of depth in which rationales are articulated. But a good deal of this process may occur at the intrapersonal rather than the interpersonal level. In other words, when exposed interpersonally to political views noticeably different from their own, people may be prompted to think about the reasons that may have led those others to hold such views.[14] This mental rehearsal of thoughts and search for rationales may occur even when the discussants do not explicitly articulate such reasons themselves.[15]

The third proposed benefit embedded in arguments about the importance of cross-cutting exposure is that it should lead to greater political tolerance. On initial consideration, this assertion sounds very similar to Allport's classic intergroup contact hypothesis, which suggests that face-to-face interaction among members of different groups can, under certain conditions, reduce prejudice.[16] At some points in its long research history, the contact hypothesis has been said to produce mixed evidence at best,[17] but more recent assessments suggest that intergroup contact usually does have positive effects, even when the situation does not meet all of the conditions enumerated by Allport and subsequent researchers.[18] Moreover, many of the additional necessary conditions tacked on in subsequent research turn out to be facilitating, but not essential, conditions.[19]

The hundreds of studies on intergroup contact have also resolved the question of causal direction by incorporating experimental studies in which contact is systematically manipulated. These studies unambiguously demonstrate that contact reduces prejudice, but not surprisingly, prejudice also lessens the amount of intergroup contact people have outside the laboratory. In a 2005 review of intergroup contact studies, Brown and Hewstone conclude that "there is now ample evidence to support his [Allport's] basic contentions."[20]

Given that intergroup contact theory has not generally been applied to contacts involving those of differing political views, the plausibility of this framework for understanding more fluidly defined groups

---

[14] Mutz (1998).
[15] Burnstein & Sentis (1981); Burnstein, Vinokur, & Trope (1973).
[16] Allport (1954).
[17] Amir (1976).
[18] Pettigrew (1998); Pettigrew & Tropp (2000).
[19] Pettigrew & Tropp (2000).
[20] Brown & Hewstone (2005, p. 256).

is worth considering. Accumulated research suggests that among the various types of "groups" that one might consider in studies of intergroup contact, contact among those of differing political views is a type ideally situated to produce beneficial effects from cross-cutting exposure. This is because the ideal sequence of events for purposes of promoting beneficial effects is one in which people first get to know one another as individuals and only later recognize each other as members of a disliked group.[21] People's political views are seldom obvious upon first meeting, and conversations about politics do not occur with sufficient regularity that people always know when they are in the company of people who hold cross-cutting views. Thus a person may easily develop a liking for another person long before discovering their differences of political opinion.

Intergroup contact findings also support the possibility that exposure to everyday differences of political opinion may translate to an appreciation of the need to tolerate differences of political opinion among disparate groups within the larger society. In linking cross-cutting exposure to political tolerance, it must be acknowledged that the kind of individual or group whom a given person might be asked to tolerate on civil libertarian grounds – perhaps an atheist, socialist, homosexual, and so forth – would seldom turn out to be exactly the same kind of person of opposing views whom one had encountered at work or in the neighborhood. This would seem to limit potential beneficial effects of cross-cutting political networks on political tolerance.

But within the large literature on intergroup contact, a smaller group of studies of "generalized intergroup contact" confirms that contact across group lines can generalize to reduce prejudice even toward outgroups that are *not* part of the intergroup contact.[22] In other words, people who have had to learn how to "agree to disagree" in their daily lives better understand the need to do so as a matter of public policy. For example, in support of the generalizability of contact effects, the extent of interpersonal contact across lines of religion, race, social class, culture, and nationality has been found to predict nonprejudicial attitudes toward groups not involved in the contact, even when taking into account potential reciprocal influences.[23] Moreover, the extent of

---

[21] Pettigrew (1997).
[22] Reich & Purbhoo (1975); Cook (1984); Pettigrew (1997); Weigert (1976).
[23] Pettigrew (1997).

contact across lines of difference also generalizes to immigration policy preferences, a more policy-oriented outcome similar to tolerance
measures. Although studies of intergroup contact have tended to use
prejudicial attitudes as their dependent variables, their findings also
appear to generalize to perspective-taking ability.[24] In other words,
cross-cutting contact improves people's abilities to see issues from the
perspectives of others, even when they personally do not agree. Reducing prejudice is clearly not the same as increasing levels of tolerance:
reducing prejudice involves altering negative attitudes toward groups,
whereas encouraging political tolerance involves increasing support for
their civil liberties *in spite of* ongoing negative attitudes. Nonetheless,
there is sufficient conceptual overlap for these literatures to be relevant
to one another.

Beyond the assumptions of political theory, and the psychological
studies of intergroup contact, quite a few empirical relationships have
been attributed to exposure to non–like-minded political perspectives.
For example, in his classic study of tolerance, Stouffer suggested that
exposure to conflicting viewpoints was the main reason that education
and tolerance were so closely connected:

Schooling *puts a person in touch with people whose ideas and values are different from one's own.* And this tends to carry on, after formal schooling is
finished, through reading and personal contacts.... To be tolerant, one has
to learn further not only that people with different ideas are not necessarily
bad people but also that it is vital to America to preserve this free market
place.... The first step in learning this may be merely to encounter the strange
and the different.[25]

Although other explanations for the education–tolerance relationship
have been proposed in subsequent research, most later studies also
reference the idea that education "increase(s) awareness of the varieties
of human experience that legitimize wide variation in . . . values."[26] The
extent to which people are exposed to differing views also has been
invoked in explanations for why women tend to be less tolerant than
men, and why those in urban environments are more tolerant than

---

[24] Reich & Purbhoo (1975).
[25] Stouffer (1955, p. 127), emphasis in original.
[26] Nunn, Crockett, & Williams (1978, p. 61).

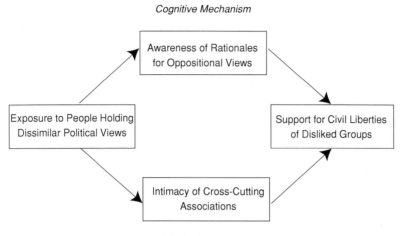

FIGURE 3.1. Potential cognitive and affective mechanisms for effects of exposure to oppositional political views on political tolerance.

those in rural areas.[27] In both cases, the assumption is that exposure to people of differing views causes urban dwellers (who live in more diverse residential environments) and men (who are more likely to work outside the home) to be more tolerant of differences.

Interpretations of political tolerance levels have stressed the diversity of people's contacts, but the extent to which people experience political conversations across lines of difference has seldom been measured in these studies. Nonetheless, closely related concepts support the likelihood of such an impact. For example, a personality dimension known as *openness to experience* is strongly positively related to tolerance,[28] and authoritarians have been found to live relatively sheltered lives with little exposure to alternative lifestyles and beliefs.[29] In a 1999 study of Russian social networks, Gibson also found that support for democratic institutions was correlated with the number of "weak ties" (i.e., nonrelatives) in a person's social network.[30]

As illustrated in Figure 3.1, there are at least two mechanisms by which exposure to oppositional political viewpoints may lead to

[27] Stouffer (1955); Sullivan, Piereson, & Marcus (1982); Nunn et al. (1978).
[28] Marcus, Sullivan, Theiss-Morse, & Wood (1995).
[29] Altemeyer (1997).
[30] Gibson (1999).

political tolerance. First, cross-cutting interactions may convey information about dissimilar others. Through what psychologists have
dubbed the process of *deprovincialization,* people learn that their
norms, customs, and lifestyles are not the only ones.[31] To the extent
that cross-cutting exposure leads to greater awareness of rationales for
oppositional views, such awareness should give people good reasons
for upholding the civil liberties of those with whom they personally
disagree; one sees that there are at least legitimate reasons for such
views, even if one personally finds them uncompelling. The top half of
Figure 3.1 illustrates this proposed chain of events whereby exposure
to people of differing political views increases awareness of rationales
for differing viewpoints and thus increases political tolerance. This link
is further supported by theorists such as Mead and Piaget who stressed
the importance of perspective-taking ability to attitudes and behaviors that subordinate the self's perspective to the larger society[32] – as
political tolerance clearly does.

In addition to this cognitive mechanism for translating cross-cutting
exposure to political tolerance, a second potential mechanism empha-
sizes affect over cognition. To paraphrase Stouffer, one can learn from
personal experience that those different from one's self are not necessarily bad people.[33] According to this mechanism, the content and
extent of people's political discussions are less important than the quality of the personal relationships that develop. It is not important that
they learn about the rationales for one another's political views, but
it is important that they develop close relationships with those they
know to hold quite different political viewpoints. Once formed, these
cross-cutting relationships make people less likely to support restric-
tions on the civil liberties of those with differing views. The bottom half
of Figure 3.1 illustrates how exposure to people of differing political
views may lead to more intimate cross-cutting associations, and thus
greater tolerance.[34]

---

[31] Pettigrew (1997, p. 174).

[32] Mead (1934); Piaget (1932).

[33] Stouffer (1955).

[34] Similar distinctions have been made in the past between "cognitive and affective bases
of political tolerance judgments" (see Kuklinski, Riggle, Ottati, Schwarz, & Wyer
1991; Theiss-Morse, Marcus, & Sullivan 1993), but in their experiments a cognitive
basis means that people are induced to think about their tolerance judgments, as
opposed to thinking about rationales for the opposing view, as suggested by the
cognitive mechanism in this study.

To summarize, interactions involving exposure to conflicting views have been assumed to benefit people largely (1) by encouraging a deeper understanding of one's own viewpoint, (2) by producing greater awareness of rationales for opposing views, and (3) by contributing to greater tolerance. If exposure to cross-cutting political views increases tolerance via its effects on awareness of rationales for oppositional points of view, then this would lend credibility to the cognitive interpretation of the benefits of cross-cutting contact. If close personal relationships across lines of political difference influence tolerance levels, then this would provide support for the affective mechanism.

Evidence from Social Networks

To examine these possibilities, I first used the same political network surveys shown in Chapter 2. Given that the extent of discussion with politically dissimilar and similar discussion partners is not a zero-sum situation whereby more discussion with agreeable partners must lead to less discussion with partners who disagree, I created separate measures of the frequency of discussion with politically like-minded and non–like-minded partners.[35]

Although the impact of discussions with *like-minded* others is not my central focus, I included this variable in my analyses in order to sort out effects that may be attributed to political discussion in general, as opposed to discussions that cross lines of political difference in particular. Moreover, since political discussion of all types is likely to occur among those more politically interested, knowledgeable, and involved, controls are also included for these predispositions. To the extent that the effects of exposure to dissimilar political views are unique and not attributable to contact that involves political agreement or to political interest and involvement more generally, then the benefits suggested by so many theorists gain support. In order to evaluate the affective mechanism, the survey also included items that made it possible to tap the level of intimacy within dyads. For each respondent, separate measures represented levels of intimacy with politically like-minded and non–like-minded discussion partners.

To serve as dependent variables for tests of the effects of cross-cutting exposure on awareness of rationales for own and for opposing political

---

[35] These measures are only weakly positively correlated.

perspectives, open-ended questions were used to solicit issue-specific rationales for three separate controversies. These included preferences among the 1996 presidential candidates, opinions about affirmative action for women and minorities, and opinions about state versus federal control of the welfare system. Based on a pretest, these issues were chosen because they were current at the time the survey was done, and thus formed a likely basis for tapping awareness that could result from recent political discussions. They are also issues for which substantial controversy exists and thus ensured participation of respondents with differing views on both sides of the issues. Respondents were asked what reasons they could think of for each of the various viewpoints ("Regardless of your own views, what reasons can you think of for . . . ?"). In other words, they were asked to view the issues through the eyes of the opposition, as well as from their own perspective. The order in which own and opposing view questions appeared was randomized to prevent potential order effects. The open-ended responses were later coded into individual rationales by two independent coders.

   Volunteered rationales for own and opposing views were not evaluated by any external standards of sophistication. But coders did eliminate from the counts the rationales that served to *delegitimize* the other viewpoint. For example, if a respondent explained why others supported Bill Clinton with reference to negative personal traits of the opinion holder ("Other people might vote for him because they are stupid") or negative traits of Clinton ("He's so slippery and slick and a good puppet"), then these were not counted as acknowledgments of a *legitimate* basis for the oppositional viewpoint.[36]

   As shown in Figure 3.2, the number of rationales that people could give for their own positions were, not surprisingly, significantly higher than those they could give for opposing views. The means were significantly different, and the measures of rationales for the two sides of a given issue were, also not surprisingly, significantly correlated with one another, thus indicating general knowledge of or interest in politics or perhaps in these specific issues. Three different issues were used to get a broader sense of a given person's knowledge of dissimilar viewpoints than one issue alone would make possible, but these were then combined into two additive indices representing a person's overall

---

[36] The reliability of coding was quite high. See Mutz (2002b) for details.

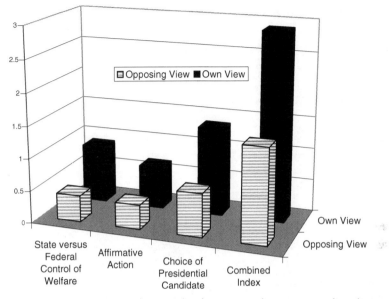

FIGURE 3.2. Awareness of rationales for own and opposing political views. (Note: At the individual level, rationales for own and opposing views are consistently significantly correlated with one another [p < .001 in all cases]. However, the group means are also consistently significantly different from one another [p < .001 in all cases]).

awareness of rationales for oppositional views and overall awareness of rationales for his or her own viewpoints.

Political tolerance was measured by using Sullivan, Piereson, and Marcus's content-controlled method, whereby respondents first volunteer their "least-liked" group and are then asked a series of six questions about extending civil liberties to these particular groups, including the extent to which they should be banned or outlawed, be allowed to hold rallies in their city, be allowed to teach in public schools, and be subject to government phone tapping.[37]

Effects on Awareness of Rationales for Own and Oppositional Views

The first hope of advocates of greater network diversity is that exposure to conflicting views will benefit citizens either by familiarizing them with legitimate reasons for holding opposing viewpoints or by

[37] Sullivan, Piereson, & Marcus 1982.

deepening their understanding of their own views by needing to defend them to others and/or to themselves. Multivariate regressions examined these two questions, one equation predicting awareness of rationales for one's own side of the issues, the second predicting awareness of rationales for the opposing viewpoints. In addition to the variables included to control for general levels of political interest, knowledge, and extremity of opinions, I included the variable representing awareness of rationales on the other side of these same issues. Those with high interest in these three particular issues are obviously likely to score high on both measures. So in analyses predicting awareness of rationales for oppositional views, awareness of rationales for one's own views also was included, and for the analysis predicting rationales for own views, awareness of rationales for opposing views was included. I did not assume a specific causal direction between awareness of rationales for own and awareness for others' views, but I included these variables so as to conduct a more stringent test.[38] Because awareness of rationales for oppositional perspectives and awareness of rationales for one's own views are highly correlated (because of issue-specific interest and knowledge), each of these variables served as a powerful control for the equation in which the other was the dependent variable. Also as expected, political knowledge was a positive predictor of political awareness of either variety, and extremity of political views had predictable effects, increasing awareness of rationales for one's own views, while reducing the number of rationales that could be offered for others' views.

For purposes of evaluating the claim that cross-cutting exposure contributes to a deeper understanding of one's own views and/or to a greater awareness of rationales for oppositional views, Figure 3.3 shows the independent effects of exposure to agreement and disagreement on awareness of rationales for one's own and oppositional political perspectives. The left-side panel of Figure 3.3 illustrates the impact of political disagreement. As shown by the top line in Figure 3.3, counter to what theorists such as Mill have proposed, there was no compelling evidence that exposure to non–like-minded views

---

[38] Including these variables was important in order to eliminate potential confounding with characteristics linked to issue-specific knowledge for the three issues used to create measures of awareness of rationales for own and others' views.

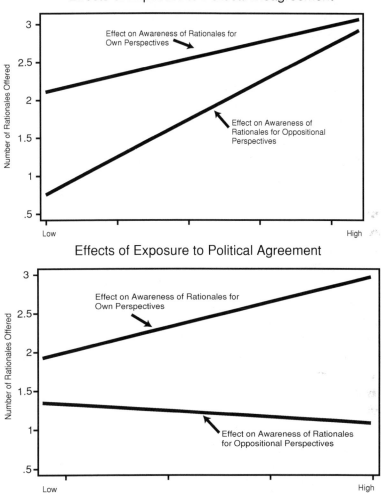

FIGURE 3.3. Effects of exposure to political agreement and disagreement on awareness of rationales for own and oppositional political perspectives.

had an impact on awareness of rationales for people's *own* political perspectives. Even when examined among the most likely subgroups within the population (such as those who have strongly held views or high levels of education), there is no evidence that those with more diverse political networks have thought through their own positions more thoroughly as a result of exposure to oppositional views.

However, consistent with the idea that people learn about *opposi-tional* views from cross-cutting contact, the bottom line on the left-hand side of Figure 3.3 shows that, all else being equal, exposure to oppositional viewpoints significantly increases awareness of legitimate rationales for opposing views. The steep lower line in Figure 3.3 shows that exposure to oppositional viewpoints is particularly important for purposes of familiarizing people with legitimate reasons for viewpoints that differ from their own. All else being equal in terms of political interest, knowledge, attitude extremity, and so forth, as exposure to disagreement increases, so does awareness of rationales for perspectives other than one's own. Noticeably, at the highest levels of exposure to disagreement, respondents were aware of virtually as many rationales against their own position as for it. In theory, this should be an ideal state for a deliberative democratic citizen: he or she is thoughtfully considering a controversial political topic. Those with high levels of exposure to political disagreement would thus have more balanced judgment.[39]

How large is the effect of exposure to dissimilar views on awareness of legitimate rationales for oppositional views? From the lowest to the highest levels of disagreement reported, awareness of rationales for oppositional views more than *triples*. Given that the mean number of oppositional rationales that people could think of was 1.46, the increase due to cross-cutting networks could have quite significant consequences for the perceived legitimacy of political outcomes.

But in order to make a convincing case for this effect, it is important to establish that it is exposure to political *disagreement*, and not just political discussion in general, that is driving awareness of rationales for oppositional views. The right-hand side of Figure 3.3 thus allows us to compare the predictive power of exposure to agreement as opposed to disagreement. Exposure to agreement is not a significant predictor of awareness of rationales for own or of rationales for oppositional views. In its capacity to educate about oppositional perspectives, exposure to disagreement appears to be unique.

With cross-sectional data, how confident can one be that exposure to cross-cutting political views actually brings about greater awareness

---

[39] See Sniderman (1981) for further discussion of what it means to have "balanced judgment."

of rationales for opposing views? These analyses rule out the most obvious spurious influences. For example, because a person knows a lot about politics, he or she may be more confident of defending his or her own views and thus be more willing to engage in cross-cutting interactions as well.[40] Because the relationships survive controls for general political knowledge, interest, and awareness specific to these issues, spuriousness is less of a concern.

Nonetheless, reverse causation remains a distinct possibility. Awareness of rationales for oppositional views might lead one to feel more confident engaging in political discussions with those of opposing perspectives. The problem with this rival interpretation is that, if true, it ought to apply equally well, if not more so, to the analysis involving awareness of rationales for one's *own* views; the more deeply committed one is to his or her position, and the more supportive rationales one has in one's arsenal, the less threatened one should be by oppositional viewpoints. But awareness of rationales for one's own views *is not* related to exposure to conflicting views in one's personal network. Although the absence of this relationship represents a null finding with respect to one of the three proposed benefits, ultimately this pattern strengthens the case for the idea that exposure to conflicting views contributes to greater awareness of legitimate rationales for opposing views.

In one sense, the significant impact of these measures of cross-cutting exposure is surprising because they do not incorporate the more specific requirements many theorists deem necessary, such as a level of mutual respect or civility. In Figure 3.4, I use this same model to see whether an additional stipulation of this kind makes any difference. Does civility in interaction help generate more beneficial outcomes from cross-cutting political dialogue? Drawing on scales widely used to classify long-term patterns of communication within families, a *civil* orientation to conflict was defined as one that combines an acknowledgment of the importance of expressing dissenting views with an emphasis on social harmony. In other words, a civil orientation is one that does not duck conflict entirely, but that simultaneously embraces the importance of maintaining harmonious social relationships.

As shown in Figure 3.4, people who have a civil orientation toward conflict are particularly likely to benefit from exposure to

[40] Conover & Searing (1998).

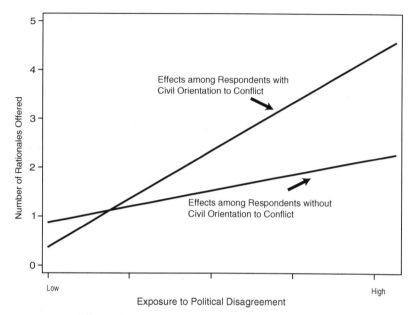

FIGURE 3.4. Effects of exposure to oppositional views on awareness of rationales for oppositional viewpoints, by orientation to conflict.

non–like-minded views. Taking this interaction into account strengthens the overall explanation of awareness of oppositional perspectives. The size of the effect among members of this group is more than twice the size of the effect on those without a civil orientation. Those who value both frank opinion expression *and* social harmony get the most out of their cross-cutting interactions. Just as theorists have suggested, civility clearly makes a difference in extracting maximal benefits from cross-cutting networks, though civility does not appear to be a necessary condition for benefits to occur.

Consequences for Political Tolerance

Figure 3.1 proposed two mechanisms for translating exposure to oppositional political views into political tolerance. If the affective ties between people of opposing political views are what is important for purposes of translating cross-cutting ties into political tolerance, then one would expect closeness within politically heterogeneous relationships to be particularly important to political tolerance. If the cognitive benefits are primary, then people's awareness of rationales for others' views should be most predictive of political tolerance.[41]

In evaluating this model, I also took into account the possibility that tolerance might have reciprocal effects with each of these key predictors. More tolerant people may be more likely to form close relationships with those of differing political views and/or may be more likely as a result of their tolerance to be open to learning about reasons for others' views. But even taking those possibilities into account, I found both the cognitive and affective mechanisms shown in Figure 3.1 to be at work translating exposure to dissimilar views into greater political tolerance. Closer relationships across lines of difference *and* greater knowledge of rationales for these differences predicted tolerance, even after controlling for political knowledge, political interest, extremity of issue opinions, and so forth. Interestingly, awareness of rationales for one's own views did *not* contribute significantly to political tolerance. Despite the fact that the two measures were highly correlated, awareness of rationales for own and opposing views represent distinctly different types of knowledge with very different consequences.

As shown in Figure 3.5, the size of the cognitive and affective effects on tolerance was modest, and the two effects were very similar in size. But together they produced a sizable effect on tolerance. If one generally perceives those opposed to one's own views to have some legitimate, if not compelling reasons for being so, then one will be more likely to extend the rights of speech, assembly, and so forth, to disliked groups. Likewise, close ties with those who hold differing political views increase tolerance. These effects are not merely a function of attitude extremity or general or issue-specific forms of political knowledge, as all of these considerations were accounted for in the model.

What then is the size of the net impact of cross-cutting exposure on political tolerance? Considered separately, the cognitive mechanism suggests that if all else remained constant, a person who had the highest levels of exposure to oppositional views would score just over 4 percent higher on the tolerance scale than someone who had the lowest

---

[41] For details on this analysis, see Mutz (2002b). As it turns out, the coefficients are virtually identical when reciprocal causation is taken into account.

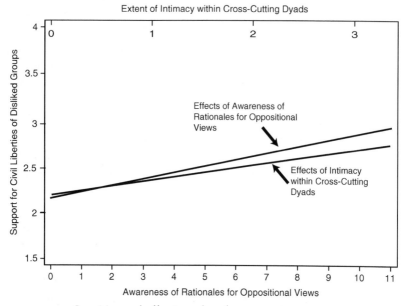

FIGURE 3.5. Cognitive and affective roles of cross-cutting exposure.

levels of exposure to oppositional views. Thus the magnitude of the cognitive mechanism is small by most standards. When considered on its own, the corresponding size of the affective mechanism is just over an 11 percent increase in tolerance from those least to most exposed to cross-cutting political views. Given that these effects are simultaneous, the total impact from cross-cutting exposure is to raise tolerance by just over 15 percent. These findings thus lend some credibility to the many claims of democratic theorists about the benefits of cross-cutting exposure.

Although the size of these relationships is modest, they are more impressive if one takes into consideration the large amount of noise in the operational measures relative to the concepts they represent. Ideally, for example, one would want a measure of awareness of legitimate rationales for oppositional views that takes into account *all* potential controversies. Instead, this larger concept is represented here by only three political controversies. Likewise, the measure of the extent to which people's networks involve cross-cutting exposure has been limited by constraining respondents to only three discussants, when a more extensive network battery might include a greater number of weak ties.

The type of contact examined in this book is by its very nature infrequent and often fleeting, and thus quite difficult to measure.

I also abandon stringent assumptions about the *kind* of exposure to cross-cutting views that is important. I do not assume that when exposed to conflicting views people must truly "deliberate" according to any particular theoretical definition; nor do I assume that when people are exposed to conflicting views the context is one in which people have equal status, reciprocity, and so forth. Exposure to oppositional political views requires only that people talk politics with someone who has political views that are to some recognizable degree different from their own (and vice versa for exposure to like-minded views). Even though this is a far cry from what theorists and others envision as the *most* beneficial, exposure to conflicting views – even at the minimalist level defined here – appears to have the capacity to produce some beneficial effects.

Replication of these analyses on other data sets would be a natural next step to increase confidence in the findings. But unfortunately, as mentioned earlier in this chapter, there are no other national surveys addressing both the constitution of Americans' political networks and levels of political tolerance. The General Social Surveys have at times included both tolerance measures and social network measures, but there is no information available about *political* agreement or disagreement among discussion partners. Other social network data sets make it possible to examine the extent of political agreement and disagreement within networks,[42] but they do not include tolerance judgments.[43]

An Experimental Confirmation

Given the lack of other data for purposes of replication, and recognizing that statistical techniques can only go so far in strengthening causal inferences, I subjected one key part of this model to an additional experimental test. Ideally, I would test all of the relationships shown in Figure 3.1 in a controlled laboratory environment, manipulating exposure to cross-cutting political views and observing the consequences.

---

[42] Huckfeldt & Sprague (1995a); Dalton, Beck, Huckfeldt, & Koetzle (1998).
[43] See Gibson (1999) for similar data on social networks and tolerance in Russia.

However, for the bottom half of Figure 3.1, that is, the affective mechanism, an experimental design is simply not feasible. At least within the context of a short-term laboratory experiment, one cannot prompt people to forge cross-cutting friendships and evaluate the effects of their intimacy.

But the cognitive mechanism shown in the top half of Figure 3.1 is amenable to experimentation. Although it is not possible to simulate the effects of ongoing, accumulated exposure to cross-cutting political viewpoints in a laboratory setting, even a large, one-time exposure to the rationales behind many perspectives different from one's own could simulate this experience. If one learns from such an experience that those who have views different from one's own have their reasons, despite the fact that one may disagree with them, such exposure should promote support for the general principle of tolerance.

For these purposes, I used a three-group experimental design in which eighty-two student subjects were randomly assigned to receive a large dose of political views that were either consistent with their preexisting views, contrary to their preexisting views, or irrelevant to their political views (the control group). While waiting to participate, all subjects filled out a pretest questionnaire that asked for demographic and political information as well as opinions on eight different controversial issues. These included the death penalty, same sex marriage, the use of mammals in medical research, affirmative action for women and minorities, the emphasis in sex education programs on abstinence versus birth control and sexually transmitted disease prevention, vouchers for private and parochial schools, stricter environmental policies, and hate crime laws. In addition, scales were included to tap individuals' personality characteristics including perspective-taking ability[44] and dogmatism.[45] Dogmatism is a stable personality trait known to predict political tolerance. Although perspective-taking ability has not been studied in relation to political tolerance, measuring it in this theoretical context makes sense because it represents the capacity to entertain others' points of view, as suggested by the purely cognitive mechanism in the upper half of Figure 3.1. The perspective-taking scale represents a cognitive, nonemotional form of empathy and is not related to

[44] See Davis (1983).
[45] See Altemeyer (1997).

empathy's emotional components.[46] Both Piaget and Mead stressed the importance of perspective-taking capability for behavior that subordinates the self's perspective to the larger society, as tolerance certainly does.[47] This capacity should condition people's ability to appreciate the legitimacy of conflicting political perspectives. Exposure to cross-cutting political perspectives combined with perspective-taking ability should provide a particularly good reason for upholding others' rights to speech, assembly, and so forth.

After the pretest, each subject was exposed to rationales for oppositional or like-minded views, or to nothing at all. Because the cognitive mechanism in Figure 3.1 hypothesizes a purely *informational* effect from cross-cutting exposure on tolerance, the manipulation was limited to conveying information about arguments behind oppositional or like-minded positions, without any face-to-face contact with another human being. Further, because this theory concerns the effects of *generalized* exposure to contradictory views on tolerance, and not effects of exposure to any one topic or area of controversy, all subjects were exposed to either multiple rationales for multiple political viewpoints that matched their own, rationales for views they were known to oppose, or no new information in the control group. To strengthen the manipulation, exposure to like-minded or non–like-minded views was carried out by exposing respondents to consistently agreeable or disagreeable arguments for three separate issues. In order to make certain results would not depend upon arguments surrounding any one issue or controversy, a randomized schedule dictated for which of the eight different pretest issue controversies each subject received stimuli (either agreeable or disagreeable) and the order in which the issues were received.[48]

In both experimental conditions, three brief "assignments" provided a pretext for exposing people to rationales in support of, or in opposition to, their own views. For each assignment, subjects were given a stack of five index cards, each bearing a rationale in support of one particular issue position. The first assignment asked subjects to order the

---

[46] Davis (1983).

[47] Piaget (1932); Mead (1934).

[48] If a subject chose the midpoint on the scale, another issue was substituted according to a random schedule.

cards by strength of argument from strongest to weakest, and then to copy them onto a separate sheet of paper; the second assignment asked the subject to imagine himself or herself as a speechwriter for a political candidate endorsing that particular issue position and to embed the arguments into a speech written for the candidate; the third assignment simply replicated the first one but with a third issue.[49] So in total each experimental subject in a treatment condition was exposed to fifteen arguments concerning three different issue positions, all of which were either systematically consistent with or inconsistent with some of the many political views the subject had expressed in the pretest. The goal of the assignments was to encourage subjects to process all of the rationales on the cards fully, and copying them and thinking about them are known to facilitate this process. After completing the assignments, a posttest was administered that included a "content-controlled" measure of political tolerance virtually identical to the one administered by telephone in the social network survey.

The raw mean comparisons resulting from this experiment were in the expected direction with lower tolerance in the control condition relative to the oppositional views condition, but none of the differences among the three groups was significant. However, when the efficiency of the comparisons was improved by taking into account subjects' political perspectives, perspective-taking ability, and levels of dogmatism, there were significant effects on tolerance among those respondents who had high perspective-taking ability. This single dose of oppositional perspectives alone was not enough to produce across-the-board effects on the sample. But as predicted, perspective-taking ability served as an important contingent condition for the effects of cross-cutting exposure. High perspective-taking ability directly encouraged greater political tolerance, so we know that those accustomed to thinking about controversies from more than one perspective also tended to be more tolerant. But more important to the purposes of the experiment, as illustrated in Figure 3.6, the experimental manipulation of exposure to rationales for oppositional views also increased political tolerance among those high in perspective-taking ability. In contrast, analyses comparing tolerance in the control group to that in the group

---

[49] For the specific wording of these assignments, see Mutz (2002b).

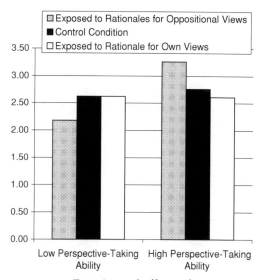

FIGURE 3.6. Experimental effects of exposure to oppositional views. (Note: All means are statistically indistinguishable except for those exposed to rationales for opposition views among the group high in perspective-taking ability. A two-factor analysis of variance confirmed a main effect for perspective-taking ability [$F = 5.90$, $p < .05$] and a significant interaction between experimental manipulation and perspective-taking ability [$F = 3.96$, $p < .05$].)

exposed to like-minded rationales showed no significant main effects or interactions.

As Figure 3.6 shows, among those high in perspective-taking ability, mean levels of tolerance were higher when subjects were exposed to rationales for oppositional views. However, among those low in perspective-taking ability, tolerance levels were *lower* when subjects were exposed to oppositional views. This pattern may result from the fact that exposing people to counterattitudinal arguments when they are not able to see things through another's eyes causes them to counterargue and strengthen their resolve, believing perhaps even more ardently that those who disagree with them are unworthy, benighted opponents.

To put the size of these effects in perspective, among those who had high perspective-taking ability, receiving exposure to rationales for non–like-minded views on three issues caused them to score about 14 percent higher on the tolerance scale. Although the small, relatively homogeneous student sample used in this experiment is by no means a representative one, that an effect of this size was generated by one single, disembodied exposure to cross-cutting political views is impressive. And again, as in the social network survey, exposure to like-minded viewpoints produced no such effects, thus confirming that is exposure to *dissimilar* views that is encouraging tolerance, rather than exposure to political argument more generally.

Benefits of Hearing the Other Side

Exposure to dissimilar views has been deemed a central element – if not the sine qua non – of the kind of political dialogue that is needed to maintain a democratic citizenry: "Democratic public discourse does not depend on pre-existing harmony or similarity among citizens ... but rather on the ability to create meaningful discourses across lines of difference."[50] The extent to which people are exposed to cross-cutting political viewpoints has become of increasing concern to observers of American politics as a result of trends toward increasing residential balkanization.[51] If people self-select into lifestyle enclaves with similar-minded others, their exposure to dissimilar political views should suffer.

Collectively these results suggest that hearing the other side plays an important role in encouraging democratic values by familiarizing people with legitimate rationales for opposing viewpoints. Interestingly, this impact is particularly pronounced among people who care about maintaining social harmony; that is, those who engage in cross-cutting conversations, but who would remain silent rather than risk conflict that might end the association altogether.

To the extent that a trend toward residential balkanization translates into a decline in conversations across lines of political difference, one of its adverse effects may be fewer opportunities for people to learn about legitimate rationales for oppositional viewpoints. Particularly when policies or candidates other than one's own top preferences

[50] Calhoun (1988, p. 220).
[51] Harrison & Bennett (1995); Frey (1995).

carry the day, the findings in this chapter suggest that the perceived legitimacy of the winning candidates and policies may be hindered by a lack of awareness of legitimate rationales for opposing views. If people are surrounded by others who think much as they do, they will be less aware of the legitimate arguments on the other side of political controversies.

Hearing the other side is also important for its indirect contributions to political tolerance. The capacity to see that there is more than one side to an issue, that a political conflict is, in fact, a *legitimate* controversy with rationales on both sides, translates to greater willingness to extend civil liberties to even those groups whose political views one dislikes a great deal.

In addition to simply becoming aware of oppositional arguments, this mechanism is augmented by influence that flows through the affective ties that people maintain across lines of political difference. If my best friend is politically very different from me, this personal tie will contribute to greater political tolerance, even if our conversations seldom include political arguments. It is interesting to note that from this perspective, the fact that Americans seldom discuss politics in any great depth is probably a feature rather than a liability. Because politics is such a small part of most people's day-to-day lives, when they come into contact with people of opposing views, it is relatively easy to ignore this dimension of difference, or to discover it late enough that a friendship of some kind has already been initiated or well established. Political views need not be at the forefront of daily life or daily conversation in order to produce beneficial consequences.

Moreover, the positive role played by affective ties to politically dissimilar others suggests a need to reconsider the role of emotion in democratic judgment. Particularly in research on political tolerance, there is a tendency to think of emotion as something that promotes intolerance and prejudicial reactions to others.[52] Although evidence on this point remains inconclusive, the emotional versus deliberative citizen dichotomy often fails to acknowledge that through social interaction people form relationships that have affective components, as well as forming cognitions about information that is conveyed.

---

[52] cf. Kuklinski et al. (1991); Theiss-Morse et al. (1993).

In the analyses in this chapter, I have attempted to separate network characteristics such as intimacy in relationships, frequency of political talk, and extent of political agreement for analytic purposes. But in the real world, the network characteristics that I have separated for analytical purposes are inextricably intertwined. People generally feel closer to those who share their values, political and otherwise, and talk more frequently with those to whom they are close. Thus efforts to increase exposure to disagreement may necessitate trade-offs in other network characteristics that are also generally valued. For example, in order to increase levels of exposure to oppositional views in the population, people will need to have a greater number of weak ties and probably less intimacy on average within their networks.

Although trust has not been directly examined here, it goes hand in hand with homogeneity of views.[53] Dense networks of tight-knit social relationships and their characteristic high levels of trust may form at the expense of exposure to cross-cutting views. Close relationships obviously have their virtues, but large pluralistic societies such as the United States undoubtedly need citizens with a good number of weak ties in their social networks in order to sustain support for democratic freedoms in the midst of such great heterogeneity.[54]

Ultimately, political tolerance is about formalized ways in which people agree to disagree. It is primarily about restraint and not doing, rather than political action. Thus carrying on conversations across lines of political difference, conversations in which one must agree to disagree at a microlevel, may teach important lessons about the necessity of political tolerance. After all, political tolerance is just the macrolevel, public policy rendition of agreeing to disagree.

In this book I have purposely isolated one particular aspect of the deliberative encounter, the extent of cross-cutting exposure, and examined its consequences using both survey and experimental evidence. Although advantageous in some respects, this narrowness also limits the scope of the conclusions that should be drawn from it. Does the composition of people's social networks have meaningful consequences for political tolerance and democratic legitimacy? My answer

---

[53] Gibson (1999); Baldassare (1985).
[54] Simmel (1955); Karatnycky (1999).

to this question is yes, on the basis of evidence to date. Although these findings do not support the argument that more deliberation per se is what American politics needs most, the findings lend supporting evidence to claims about the benefits of one central tenet of deliberative theory: that the perspectives people advocate when they talk about politics must be contested.

4

The Dark Side of Mixed Political Company

When social scientists talk about the consequences of communication across lines of difference, what they generally have in mind are the potential *benefits* that may accrue from face-to-face interactions of this kind, the very kind outlined in the previous chapter. Or perhaps they are concerned with the potential dangers posed by a lack of political diversity in people's social environments. In either case, social integration is seen as a public good, whereas segregation is inherently bad; heterogeneous environments are perceived to be ideal for promoting democratic ends, and homogeneous ones are considered undesirable.

And yet, when broadly considered, plenty of evidence points to the potential for *negative* outcomes as a result of communication across lines of political difference. Most often, this evidence is taken from studies of small groups in which polarization results from bringing those of opposing views together for discussion. If cross-cutting contact produces defensiveness or causes people to dig in their heels and counterargue, they may become all that much more strongly committed to their original positions, thus making further conversation and compromise even more difficult. This same "dark side" has been noted in considerations of the supposed benefits of "deliberation" variously defined. Still other scholars note that violence can and sometimes does erupt when those of differing views come into close contact. The threat of a violent outcome is particularly great when those who have been living in segregated settings are first exposed to those of differing views.

The most ardent critics of the idea that anything beneficial might result from a communication process of this kind are Hibbing and Theiss-Morse, who argue in *Stealth Democracy* that deliberation is either bad for, or, at the very least, not beneficial for democracy.[1] They base their argument on evidence from voluntary associations and from planned deliberative events in which diverse people are brought together to interact, with the goal of reaching consensus. Consistent with my findings, they suggest that voluntary groups tend to avoid potentially controversial topics in favor of more practical tasks,[2] thus giving members a diminished appreciation for the difficulty of reaching a conclusion when handling divisive issues. Hibbing and Theiss-Morse argue further that even planned deliberative events do not produce beneficial consequences.[3] Other assessments of this literature suggest some benefits under some conditions, but not under others.[4]

My own observations generally concur with Hibbing and Theiss-Morse's in some respects. As discussed in Chapter 2, many people do not like conflict and prefer not to talk about politics with those who have conflicting views. But I diverge from their conclusion, which suggests that because people generally do not like it, we should not worry too much about whether it happens. I dislike arguments with my husband, but I cannot, as a consequence, claim we would be better off not having them. Keeping differences under wraps for fear that they might endanger a relationship can have dire consequences, for couples as well as for countries. Hibbing and Theiss-Morse see democracy as threatened by open displays of conflict and consider it dangerous to have conflict out in the open. In contrast, I would argue that the more it is a habitual part of people's ongoing interactions with others, the less likely it is to erupt into something truly dangerous.

To be fair, although Hibbing and Theiss-Morse make some strong statements about why deliberation per se is a waste of time, they never suggest that all of people's informal conversations about politics are similarly worthless, particularly conversations that take place among those of differing views. In their critique, they are referring primarily

[1] Hibbing & Theiss-Morse (2002).
[2] Eliasoph (1998).
[3] Hibbing & Theiss-Morse (2002).
[4] See Mendelberg (2002).

to situations in which people must reach a *conclusion* of some kind as a result of their interactions. In most real world scenarios, the group or dyad does not need to reach a consensus; the talk occurs for its own sake, without any end result in mind.[5]

Regardless of one's views on the merits of deliberation, promoting informal political talk among people of differing views remains popular both in theory and in practice. At the same time, some scholars reluctantly acknowledge that certain groups or individuals who have clashing views are probably best kept apart, as face-to-face contact is no cure-all for intensely held differences of opinion.

But the "dark side" I mention in the chapter title is not about failed cross-cutting interactions; instead it refers to situations in which cross-cutting exposure *succeeds* in making people more aware of oppositional views. It even succeeds in making them more tolerant of oppositional political perspectives. But it nonetheless entails significant costs for what democracies generally value.

Failure through Success: The Political Costs of Mixed Company

In all of the examples provided thus far, the potential for negative outcomes from cross-cutting exposure occurs strictly because cross-cutting contact has *failed* to produce the benefits that deliberative theory and intergroup contact ideally might bring about. For example, if conversations across lines of difference lead participants to polarize their positions, then cross-cutting exposure has failed to create mutual understanding. Likewise, if contact among members of different groups only brings about greater animosity and resentment, then communication across lines of difference has failed to improve intergroup relations.

In contrast, this chapter examines the potential for an undesirable outcome that occurs as a result of the *success* of cross-cutting exposure in giving people of opposing perspectives an understanding of the other side's views. Although the potential benefits of these interactions have received the most attention, other theories hint at the potential drawbacks of cross-cutting exposure for one democratic outcome in particular – political participation.

---

[5] Schudson (1997) makes this point about the difference between conversations that are deliberative and goal-oriented versus those which occur purely for pleasure.

Within political science, exposure to those of differing political perspectives was first raised to the status of a research concept under the designation of "cross-pressures." Authors of some of the earliest research on American elections voiced concerns about the potentially deleterious impact of cross-pressures, defined as the presence of people of inconsistent political views within an individual's social environment.

Interest in cross-pressures emerged from observations of how neatly social groups mapped onto patterns of voting behavior. Indeed, one of the strongest messages conveyed by the earliest studies of American voting was the theme of the social homogeneity of political behavior. For example, *The People's Choice* and *Voting* both stressed the *social* nature of political decisions. As Lazarsfeld and colleagues put it, "More than anything else, people can move other people."[6] They suggested that the social nature of political decisions extended not only to decisions about whether to vote for a given candidate, but also whether to participate politically at all.

The People's Choice was the first study to suggest that conflicts and inconsistencies among the factors influencing an individual's vote decision had implications for political participation: "Whatever the source of the conflicting pressures, whether from social status or class identification, from voting traditions or the attitudes of associates, the consistent result was to delay the voter's final decision."[7] Subsequently, *The American Voter* more directly acknowledged the problem of conflicting considerations surrounding political choices:

The person who experiences some degree of conflict tends to cast his vote for President with substantially less enthusiasm ... and he is somewhat less likely to vote at all than is the person whose partisan feelings are entirely consistent. ... If attitude conflict leaves its impress on several aspects of behavior it also influences what we will call the individual's involvement in the election.[8]

Likewise, Carl Hovland and colleagues suggested that the effects of conflicting social influences included "vacillation, apathy, and loss of interest in conflict-laden issues."[9]

[6] Lazarsfeld, Berelson, & Gaudet (1944, p. 171).
[7] Ibid., p. 60.
[8] Campbell, Converse, Miller, & Stokes (1960, pp. 83, 85).
[9] Hovland, Janis, & Kelley (1953, p. 283).

Cross-pressures that arise from affiliations with multiple groups had long been of interest in political sociology as well. Georg Simmel, for example, attributed great significance to the "web of affiliations" and cross-cutting social relationships, as contrasted with the highly homogeneous kinship-linked groups of an earlier era.[10] Those exposed to a variety of different cues about appropriate social and political attitudes were assumed to experience discomfort as a result, though arguments about how people resolved this discomfort varied.

More specifically, these researchers surmised that personal associations that push individuals in opposite directions with respect to their vote choices cause a kind of paralysis with respect to political action. Given that most people have multiple roles and identities, perfect consistency in the social environment is unlikely, and citizens are likely to experience varying degrees of dissonance when their various group identities have contradictory implications for their political preferences. So, for example, a citizen who was white-collar and Catholic or Protestant and a member of a labor union was assumed to be cross-pressured by this combination of religion and occupational status.

Although most research attention was focused on the instability of voting choices in cross-pressured groups, some researchers also observed that cross-pressured voters tended to make later political decisions and tended to express lower levels of political interest than those in more homogeneously supportive social environments. In most cases ascriptive group memberships – such as whether a person was employed in a white-collar or unionized occupation and whether he or she was Protestant or Catholic – served as the basis for inferring that a person was experiencing cross-pressures; in some analyses this assertion was based on the political leanings of the primary groups surrounding an individual citizen, such as friends, family, or coworkers. Although the primary interest was in which side would ultimately "win" the individual's vote, a secondary concern was the impact these conflicting influences had on levels of political involvement.

As promising as this idea seemed, the brief history of research on cross-pressures suggests that it was an intuitively appealing idea that did not survive long enough to be fleshed out into a genuine theory of

[10] Simmel (1955).

political behavior. In particular, researchers had yet to work out exactly *why* cross-pressured individuals might restrain themselves in or abstain altogether from political activity. Moreover, the popularity of the idea did not persist long enough for the kind of data that were needed to give it a fair test – information on social and *political* networks.

In this chapter, I revisit the concept of "cross-pressures" and the influence of oppositional views on participation, reviewing the nature of the original evidence, the refutation of that evidence in subsequent work, and the emergence of more recent theories that revive the basic idea behind cross-pressures in somewhat different contexts. Finally, I use data better suited to testing this hypothesis to develop a theory linking the extent of political heterogeneity in a person's social environment to levels of political participation.

Whatever Happened to Cross-Pressures?

Despite early enthusiasm, the initial interest in testing the cross-pressure hypothesis died out after subsequent analyses repeatedly failed to confirm these early findings. For example, Pool, Abelson, and Popkin looked for these effects in the 1960 national election data, but to no avail.[11] Moreover, in a reanalysis of data from the 1948 Elmira study and the 1956 national election study, Horan found that even the earlier evidence had resulted from "interpreting direct effects of social positions on nonvoting as due to a more complex cross-pressures phenomenon."[12] In other words, the investigators had unintentionally confounded the direct effects of membership in social categories with the effects of being linked to *conflicting* social categories.

Subsequent studies differed in terms of the kinds of cross-pressures that were evaluated (e.g., primary group or class-based), and whether bivariate or more complex, multivariate approaches were used,[13] but despite a promising beginning, by the late 1970s studies of cross-pressures had largely disappeared due to an accumulation of negative evidence.[14] The theory of political cross-pressures became part of "that

[11] Pool, Abelson, & Popkin (1965).
[12] Horan (1971).
[13] Jackson & Curtis (1972); Davis (1982).
[14] See Knoke (1990) for a review.

category of plausible theories whose empirical support has been cut out from under them."[15]

Although the concept was a prominent one in early voting research, the "'theory of political cross-pressures' is in fact a rather mixed bag of propositions and assumptions."[16] In fact, to call the study of cross-pressures a "theory" at all may have been a bit premature. The term has been used interchangeably to refer to how people sort out their opinions in the face of conflicting social pressures, as well as how exposure to differing viewpoints alters their political participation. Because this idea evolved gradually from analysis and interpretation of data, it has often lacked clarity as an abstract theoretical formulation. Most versions are in agreement with the assumption that "social interaction is the primary mechanism linking social group membership and individual political behavior," but beyond this, understandings of the term have varied.[17]

Since these initial studies, scholars have learned a great deal about the kinds of social contexts conducive to political participation. The link between the composition of people's social environments and political participation is now widely acknowledged. For example, studies of social contexts and social networks have reached a consensus on the idea that political activity is rooted in social structure. But for the most part this conclusion refers to the idea that highly participative social contexts and active social networks further enhance the prospects for an individual's political participation. Mobilization via social networks has been recognized as one of the major factors underlying turnout.[18] For example, the extent of participation within neighborhoods has consequences for the likelihood of individual participation,[19] though whether this social context affects all or only some particular kinds of participatory acts remains unclear.[20]

Whether these studies use characteristics of some larger social context (e.g., a city, county, or neighborhood) or measures of an individual's immediate social network to assess a person's social environment,

[15] Horan (1971, p. 659).
[16] Ibid., p. 659.
[17] Ibid., p. 650.
[18] E.g., Rosenstone & Hansen (1993); Verba, Schlozman, & Brady (1995).
[19] E.g., Huckfeldt (1979, 1986); Giles & Dantico (1982).
[20] See Kenny (1992); Leighley (1990).

the general conclusion is that a participatory social environment begets still more participation, and the mechanism assumed to account for this effect is the same in both cases; that is, the more people interact with one another within a social context, the more norms of participation will be transmitted, and the more people will be recruited into political activity.

To be sure, social interaction appears to make a difference in the extent to which individuals become politically active. But does it matter whether the interaction is comprised of like-minded people or those of dissimilar political views? Some scholars have theorized that people may be more likely to participate if their social environment is consistent with their political beliefs. For example, a study by Gimpel, Dyck, and Shaw suggests that Republicans living in more heavily Republican areas are more likely to turn out to vote than Republicans in more heterogeneous social contexts.[21] Other scholars have suggested just the opposite of this prediction; that is, that diversity (defined in the aggregate) should produce greater conflict, and heightened conflict and competitiveness should lead to greater participation.[22] Unfortunately, neither of these two groups of studies has directly addressed the cross-pressures hypothesis, that is, whether conflicting influences on an *individual* have implications for levels of political participation.

Studies suggesting that heterogeneity should increase participation are based on conceptualizations (and measures) of heterogeneity at the level of large-scale, aggregate-level social contexts. The theory in this case is that heterogeneous contexts make for more intense battles over available resources. As a result of greater competition and conflict between groups, people will perceive their participation to be more important than they would otherwise. Competitive (i.e., heterogeneous) electoral districts should thus lead to greater turnout. Oliver, for example, finds that economic diversity in cities is positively related to political participation, but strictly to participation at the local level.[23]

At the individual level, there is very limited evidence supportive of this theory, although there is plenty of evidence to suggest that

---

[21] Gimpel, Dyck, & Shaw (2004).
[22] Oliver (1999).
[23] See Oliver (2001).

discussion in general is good for participation. One exception is Leighley,[24] who operationalizes exposure to conflict in one's personal network as respondents' reports of whether a friend has tried to convince him or her to vote for a candidate of the opposite party. She finds, contrary to her hypothesis, that reported efforts to persuade are positively related to participation. But because this independent variable is an indicator of both the extent of political activity in the network and the heterogeneity of the network, separating the effects of heterogeneity and the level of political activity in the environment is difficult.

Another possibility has been suggested by Campbell, whose work incorporates expectations related to both of these theories.[25] Using aggregate-level data on the political homogeneity or heterogeneity of the counties in which respondents live, he suggests that both highly homogeneous *and* highly heterogeneous counties have higher turnout than would otherwise be predicted. In highly heterogeneous social contexts, more people participate because they want to defend their interests against the opposition. In politically homogeneous contexts, people are more likely to vote because civic norms are strong and people reinforce one another in their like-minded perspectives. Campbell finds that politically oriented attitudes and actions are most lacking in the middle of this spectrum.

Unfortunately, none of these results speaks directly to the question of individual-level cross-pressures. Although the term *cross-pressures* rarely appears in print anymore, it would be a mistake to assume that the idea itself has completely died out. On the contrary, research on public opinion has become increasingly sensitive to the impact of social context on political attitudes and behaviors, and to the social anxieties that often play a role in decisions about whether to take political action. This core idea has taken many forms. For example, in Noelle-Neumann's "spiral of silence" theory, she posits a "fear of social isolation" as the motivation for some to speak out on their political views while others fall silent with respect to their less popular views.[26]

Concerns surrounding the "social desirability" problem in survey research also suggest an awareness that social context can affect

---

[24] Leighley (1990).
[25] See Campbell (2002).
[26] Noelle-Neumann (1984).

people's political behavior in important ways. Polls may misrepresent public opinion on sensitive issues because people do not want to express unpopular or socially unacceptable views. For example, Berinsky argues that those who fear social approbation hide behind "don't know" responses in polls.[27] As he puts it, people "may bow to the social pressures of the survey interview and choose to abstain from specific questions rather than give an opinion which might paint them in an unfavorable light."[28]

Berinsky finds evidence of this in survey results that overstate actual support for efforts to integrate public schools, and in polls from the biracial 1989 New York City mayoral election, which showed far greater support for the black candidate than was actually present in the electorate. In these examples, cross-pressures emerged from a conflict between the privately held views of individuals and their perceptions of what was socially approved by others.

One of the few contemporary theories incorporating an explicit reference to the theory of cross-pressures is Campbell's clever attempt to provide a more nuanced explanation for the surge in support for congressional candidates of the president's party in presidential election years, and the subsequent decline in off years.[29] Campbell adds a layer of complexity to the basic theory of surge and decline to explain why it is that the theory often fails in predicting the behavior of electorates. He argues that part of the explanation for surge and decline lies in turnout differences that result from a cross-pressured electorate during presidential campaigns. When the short-term forces during a presidential campaign tend to favor the candidate of the opposing party, partisans of the party disadvantaged by these short-term forces are likely to be unhappy with the performance of their party's presidential candidate. The positive underlying attitude toward their party, coupled with negative information about that candidate in the information environment, makes them feel cross-pressured, which in turn makes them less likely to vote. Those supporting the losing side of the presidential race are less likely to bother voting, so they also do not vote for their party's congressional candidate. As in Berinsky's study of social desirability

---

[27] Berinsky (1999).
[28] Berinsky (1999, p. 1210).
[29] Campbell (1997).

effects, Campbell posits that nonparticipation is seized by partisans as a convenient middle choice on a scale that otherwise forces people to choose one candidate over another. Instead of defecting to the opposite party, partisans decline to support either candidate.

On the flip side, Campbell suggests that partisans who favor the presidential candidate who is winning will be especially likely to turn out to vote. Presidential campaigns always attract more voters than congressional campaigns do, but Campbell finds that it is particularly partisans of the party advantaged by short-term forces during the campaign who are "invigorated to turn out."[30] Although they may be motivated by the success of their presidential candidate, they end up also supporting their congressional candidate, and thus contribute to the surge in support for candidates of the president's party during a presidential election year. A mixed information environment is thus argued to suppress participation, and vice versa, for a homogeneous information environment.

Finally, research on social movements also indirectly makes a case for cross-pressures as a force suppressing political participation. Although the term *cross-pressures* is never explicitly mentioned, the emphasis on the importance of "connective structures" in facilitating political activism speaks directly to the importance of social networks in influencing levels of participation. As Tarrow points out, explaining political action as a function of people's individual grievances and interests is inadequate: "Although it is individuals who decide whether or not to take up collective action, it is in their face-to-face groups, their social networks, and the connective structures between them that it is most often activated and sustained."[31] There is strong empirical support for interpersonal contacts as the key source of new recruits into social movements,[32] far more support than for ideology or individual predispositions as the motivation. Surprisingly, whom you know matters more than what you believe in determining whether you participate.

A careful reading of social movement research suggests that these connective structures encourage participation *particularly when they*

---

[30] Campbell (1997, p. 174).
[31] Tarrow (1998, p. 22).
[32] Friedman & McAdam (1992); McAdam (1986).

form connections among those of similar opinion and experience. As Tarrow suggests, social networks "lower the costs of bringing people into collective action, induce confidence that they are not alone, and give broader meaning to their claims."[33] Thus it is not social networks per se that are implicated in stimulating collective action, but networks among those who are like-minded.

But how exactly do interpersonal networks draw people into political activism? And why might heterogeneous networks discourage participation as the cross-pressures hypothesis first suggested? The social movement literature casts this theory in a rational choice framework: "Refusing to respond to the call of network partners means the potential loss of all the benefits provided by that tie. These benefits may be social, such as friendship or social honor, but they may also be material. Network ties provide people with jobs, and people are tied, in network fashion, to those with whom and for whom they work."[34] Although one cannot deny that material benefits often flow from social networks, it requires a highly cynical disposition to believe that all or even the majority of people's social ties are formed on the basis of a desire for material gain. That people want to be liked by others and that they value their reputations are sufficient to explain why members of their social networks might be effective in recruiting them into participation.

Extending this argument about the social costs of not cooperating with a network partner to understand what happens when people are surrounded by those of opposing views provides a logical explanation for why heterogeneity in the network should promote avoidance of political involvement. Declaring one's self partisan in a politically mixed setting puts one in a position to potentially alienate others. Doing the same in a homogeneous environment does not incur these same risks.

One might argue that surely people are not so rash as to judge another person less favorably simply because of his or her political perspective. But plenty of evidence suggests that they do: all else being equal, people like those who hold similar views better than those who

---

[33] Tarrow (1998, p. 23).
[34] Friedman and McAdam (1992, p. 161). The authors draw on Laumann (1973) and Granovetter (1973) to support this claim.

hold dissimilar views. By declaring themselves outside or "above" politics, people avoid taking potentially controversial positions, avoid pressure from those who might attempt to change their minds, and, most importantly, they help to preserve social harmony.

But Why Revive a Discredited Idea?

If the concept of cross-pressures basically died out as an explanation for political participation, why revive it now? First, as I have pointed out, the basic theory has not so much died as been reincarnated under a variety of different labels. But even if this had not been the case, a strong argument for taking another look can be made on the basis of methodology alone. The kind of data most appropriate to testing this hypothesis have been in short supply. In the early studies, whether a person was experiencing cross-pressures was typically measured by using social category memberships such as the fact that a person was both white-collar and Catholic. Conflicts were defined purely at the level of social categories deemed *potentially* conflictual by the researchers. Actual interactions that might exert pressure on people were not documented, even though interaction was generally the microlevel process assumed to be responsible for producing cross-pressures. Today several surveys that include batteries of items on individuals' political networks make it possible to test this hypothesis in a manner that allows measurement of actual (as opposed to inferred) exposure to cross-pressures.

In addition to the availability of more appropriate data, research since the 1950s gives us a stronger basis for formulating an actual theory as to precisely why people might respond to cross-pressures by avoiding political participation. This is particularly important because without an understanding of actual mechanisms of influence, it is difficult to sort out the implications of such influence for the democratic process.

I turn next to the task of formulating explanations for such a mechanism. In order to prevent confusion with the many different formulations of the cross-pressure hypothesis and to better specify this process, I use the term *cross-cutting networks* to refer to the extent to which members of one's social network hold views different from one's own. I refer to the extent of *cross-cutting exposure* within the network to indicate the extent to which political discussions with non–like-minded others are taking place within these networks.

To Be or Not to Be Ambivalent?

There are at least two potential social psychological mechanisms that might explain why cross-cutting exposure discourages participation. First, political inaction could be induced by the ambivalence that cross-cutting exposure is likely to engender within an individual. If citizens are embedded in networks that do not reinforce their viewpoints, but instead tend to supply them with political information that challenges their views, then cross-cutting exposure could make people uncertain of their own positions with respect to issues or candidates and therefore less likely to take political action as a result. In this case it is an internal (i.e., intrapersonal) conflict that drives the effect. The chain of events leading to suppressed participation would be one in which cross-cutting exposure leads to ambivalent attitudes, which, in turn, reduce political participation because these individuals do not have views that are sufficiently definite or strong to motivate them to political action.

No character has been criticized more for inaction that results from ambivalence than Hamlet, prince of Denmark. Laurence Olivier's Hamlet is described simply as "The Prince who could not make up his mind."[35] Readers of Shakespeare's famous play have long criticized Hamlet for indecisiveness and they frequently cite that quality as the cause of his ultimate downfall. His failure to kill Claudius when he had the chance resulted in a tragic series of events that ultimately led to his own death, as well as his mother's. And yet, could one not also argue that his extensive weighing of the pros and cons was entirely appropriate under the circumstances?

Hamlet is painfully self-aware, as are many of Shakespeare's characters. His motives may be noble, but his constant questioning of himself is not practical, and he experiences a paralyzing ambivalence as a result. His slow, plodding, deliberative decision-making process produces ambivalence and leads him to act "with wings as swift as meditation," which is to say, not swiftly at all. Although Hamlet might

---

[35] See the 1948 movie production of *Hamlet*, directed by and starring Laurence Olivier.

be the poster child for the deliberative process, the price he pays for it is enormous.

In today's popular parlance, the very kind of deliberation that theorists advocate – one that involves careful, time-consuming weighing of pros and cons, and exposure to a multitude of different viewpoints – is popularly chided as the antithesis of action. As H. Ross Perot put it, "I come from an environment where, if you see a snake, you kill it." He contrasts this with the more deliberative style of corporations such as General Motors (GM): "At GM, if you see a snake, the first thing you do is go hire a consultant on snakes. Then you get a committee on snakes, and then you discuss it for a couple of years. The likely course of action is – nothing. You figure the snake hasn't bitten anybody yet, so you just let him crawl around on the factory floor."[36]

Of course, whether one sees the potential negative influence of deliberation on action as a virtue or a vice is open to debate. But Perot's comments betray our culture's mixed feelings about the process of deliberation and its limited patience with ambivalence. Scholars may advocate exposure to cross-cutting views as conducive to a superior political decision-making process, but many have their doubts about its merits. We regularly contrast the idea of a "man of action" with someone who cannot make up his mind easily. We derogatorily call such deliberative types namby-pamby, wishy-washy, navel-gazers, without much questioning whether the "man of action" has truly given careful consideration to all of his various options. Certainly the moniker "man of deliberation" carries no such positive connotations.

Likewise, contemporary corporate advice books now speak of a condition dubbed "analysis paralysis," wherein too much information gathering and too much thinking through in the style of "on the one hand, and then on the other," lead to a detrimental state of inaction. Hamlet's problems notwithstanding, the bringing together of many minds and the consideration of multiple possibilities in dealing with an issue are often seen as unnecessary and counterproductive. If truth is obvious, then why wait?[37]

---

[36] Perot made this statement as a commentary on General Motors while a board member. It is cited in Parietti (1997).

[37] See Hibbing & Theiss-Morse (2002), for more on this theme.

As advocates of democratic principles, most scholars hope that Americans are aware of, and can understand the rationales for, different sides of an issue controversy. But at the same time, we do not want them to be paralyzed by ambivalence and abandon their responsibility to participate politically, leaving so many snakes to wander the factory floor.

One recent study suggests that excessive deliberation – even of the intrapersonal variety – may produce precisely such effects when used as a means of making decisions about political candidates. In an experimental study, Barker and Hansen randomly exposed one group of voters during the 2000 election season to a complex decision-making tool that was set up as a means of helping them decide among candidates.[38] This decision-making tool was designed to encourage systematic processing of various decision criteria for purposes of improving decision quality. Control group subjects made the same political decisions but without the help of this tool.

Consistent with expectations, the knowledgeable experimental subjects who used the decision-making tool showed greater integrative complexity as a result of being induced to think more systematically about salient criteria for their decision. But importantly, they also had weaker and less consistent preferences as a result. In contrast, the less knowledgeable subjects who used the tool relied to an even greater extent on party and ideological cues for purposes of their decisions. To the extent that this experiment simulates an ideal deliberative encounter, it indicates that strong preferences may be weakened, and thus motivation for participation would be as well.

A recent resurgence of academic interest in *ambivalence* – defined as the simultaneous presence of both positive and negative considerations directed toward the same attitude object – has been noted in both qualitative and quantitative approaches to understanding political attitudes. For example, in her in-depth interviews with Americans, Hochschild noted a tremendous amount of vacillation and uncertainty in people's views, most of which appeared to be driven by competing values and considerations as applied to political questions rather than by a lack of political expertise or thought.[39] Likewise, efforts to better

---

[38] Barker & Hansen (2005).
[39] Hochschild (1981, 1993).

understand responses to survey questions have suggested that citizens' opinions are formed from competing ideas and considerations,[40] and therefore ambivalence is often difficult to distinguish from nonattitudes as typically measured.

In studies of issues ranging from race policies to abortion, ambivalence has been found to play an important role in the formation of citizens' attitudes. The consequences of political ambivalence have been less widely explored; they appear to include more moderate political positions, less certainty in political judgments,[41] delayed formation of voting intentions, and instability in candidate evaluations.[42] Ambivalence also has been tied to having more balanced or even-handed judgments about political issues.[43] For example, simultaneous awareness of conflicting considerations bearing on a given issue can lead to higher levels of "integrative complexity,"[44] which is similar to what others call having balanced judgment: "that is, an awareness that many political questions are not black and white, and a recognition that there is something to be said for 'the other side.'"[45] This condition is distinct from having a middle-of-the-road position or no position at all, though the typical approach to the measurement of political attitudes makes such distinctions difficult to observe. Although there is quite a bit of recent research on ambivalence, it has yet to be reconnected with social context, as in the original theory of cross-pressures.

Social Accountability: Political Action versus Chickening Out

Ambivalence is not, however, the only reason that exposure to differing perspectives might lead to inaction. Social accountability may also play a powerful role. In my own social environment, I have become increasingly aware of potentially offending others through even relatively innocuous political actions such as the display of bumper stickers. Until recently, my husband's car had long featured the popular Darwin fish decal, a stylized fish symbol sprouting legs. Not long after he began

---

[40] Zaller & Feldman (1992); Zaller (1992).
[41] Guge & Meffert (1998).
[42] Lavine (2001).
[43] E.g., Sniderman (1981); Guge & Meffert (1998).
[44] See Green, Visser, & Tetlock (2000).
[45] Sniderman (1981).

dropping our children off at a new school, I noticed that the fish had been carefully stripped of its legs and tail. All that was left was an eyeball-shaped emblem, staring back at me. When I asked what had happened, he surmised it had occurred in the school parking lot and was the result of someone having taken offense at the message. He guessed this on the basis of the more numerous traditional Christian fish symbols inhabiting the same parking lot. Perhaps, he suggested, it was interpreted as an attack on Christianity or on fundamentalist doctrine.

It had not previously occurred to me that a pro-Darwin decal could be interpreted as anti-Christian, nor did my husband intend it as such when he put it on the car – anticreationist perhaps, but not anti-Christian or anti–any other religion. We thought it was a humorous decal, incorporating both religious and scientific symbolism.[46]

But now that I thought about it, I realized that I did not want my children's friends and their families wrongly thinking our family was opposed to Christianity. And even if we were, I wanted my kids to have friends of a variety of political and religious persuasions, so I had no desire to offend people. But my husband still wanted his fish back, so this time he put a sushi fish decal on the car (the same shape, but with chopsticks), a more clearly apolitical, secular statement. Out of a desire to avoid offending others, and to fit into a new community, we had cleansed our bumper décor of any "taint" of ideology. This seemed to be the right thing to do at the time, to put social harmony and the consideration of others' feelings above any need we had to express ourselves, politically or otherwise. Yet it also seemed a bit silly: would my kids really have a harder time making new friends if we were assumed to be the resident atheists?

Silly or not, I do not think my reaction was unusual. People tend to care more about social harmony in their immediate face-to-face personal relationships than about the larger political world. Given the generally low levels of interest in politics, it does not take a lot to reach this threshold. Thus a second reason that cross-cutting political networks may discourage political participation is that cross-cutting networks create the need to be accountable to conflicting constituencies.

---

[46] For academic research on "meanings" that owners of fish decals attribute to it, see Lessl (1998) or Yoon (2003).

According to this explanation, the problem is not that one is *internally* conflicted over which side to support (as in the case of ambivalence), but that one feels uncomfortable taking sides in the face of multiple constituencies. The demands of social accountability create anxiety because disagreement threatens social relationships. In mixed company, there is no way to please the members of one's network and assure social harmony: "The decision maker is caught in the middle, pushed one way by part of the group, and pulled the other way by an opposing faction. The individual is forced to defend a position in what may be perceived as a 'no win' situation, in which one side will inevitably be alienated."[47]

There is already ample qualitative evidence in support of the idea that people avoid politics as a means of maintaining interpersonal social harmony. For example, in the mid-1950s, Rosenberg noted in his in-depth interviews that the threat to interpersonal harmony was a significant deterrent to political activity.[48] More recent case studies have provided further support for this thesis. In her study of New England town meetings and an alternative workplace, Mansbridge observed that conflict avoidance was an important deterrent to participation.[49] Still others have described in great detail the lengths to which people will go in order to maintain an uncontroversial atmosphere.[50] Likewise, in focus group discussions of political topics, people report being aware of, and wary of, the risks of political discussion for interpersonal relationships.[51] As one focus group participant put it, "It's not worth it . . . to try and have an open discussion if it gets them [other citizens] upset."[52]

In the early 1970s, Verba and Nie applied a similar theoretical logic to a quantitative analysis of political participation by differentiating activities on the basis of the extent to which conflict with others was involved. Their results were inconsistent on this finding,[53] but in a more recent analysis of national survey data analyzed from this same

[47] Green et al. (2000, p. 4).
[48] Rosenberg (1954–1955).
[49] Mansbridge (1980).
[50] Eliasoph (1998).
[51] Conover & Searing (1998).
[52] Ibid.
[53] Verba & Nie (1972).

theoretical perspective, people high in conflict avoidance were less likely to participate in some ways, particularly in more public participatory acts such as protesting, working on a campaign, and having political discussions.[54]

The idea that conflict avoidance discourages participation is also consistent with social psychological studies of how people handle non-political interpersonal disagreements. When a person confronted with a difference of opinion does not shift to the other person's views or persuade the person to adopt his or her own views, the most common reaction is to devalue the issue forming the basis of the conflict.[55] By devaluing politics and avoiding political controversy, people effectively resolve the problem.

One experiment aptly illustrates the problem of social accountability. Subjects were told they would be asked to justify their opinions either to a group that was in consensus on an issue or to a group with mixed views on the same issue. The subjects who anticipated the cross-pressured group engaged in many decision-evasion tactics (including buckpassing, procrastination, and exit from the situation) in order to avoid accountability to contradictory constituencies.[56] If we generalize these findings outside the laboratory, we would expect those with high levels of cross-cutting exposure in their personal networks to put off political decisions as long as possible or indefinitely, thus making their political participation particularly unlikely.

Figure 4.1 lays out the two processes of influence I have outlined thus far. The top half of the figure illustrates how cross-cutting exposure can lead to ambivalent feelings about a political decision, which subsequently leads to inaction. The lower half of Figure 4.1 shows a direct link between cross-cutting exposure and political action, as one would expect if social accountability is at work suppressing levels of political participation. In this case, one's attitudes need not be ambivalent, and it is a straightforward desire to avoid political controversy that leads one to back away from political involvement. To the extent that cross-cutting exposure demonstrates negative effects on participation, one would expect it to be a result of one or perhaps both of these influence processes.

---

[54] Ulbig & Funk (1999).
[55] E.g., Steiner (1966).
[56] Green et al. (2000).

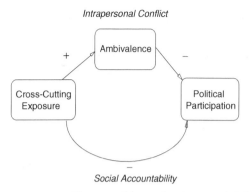

FIGURE 4.1. Two possible mechanisms explaining the effects of cross-cutting exposure on political participation.

New Evidence for an Old Theory

So what are the implications of mixed political company for political participation? And if cross-cutting exposure has negative effects on participation, is it because we are too afraid of offending our friends and neighbors, or because we just cannot make up our minds? In the analyses that follow, I first provide a general examination of the extent to which cross-cutting exposure within social networks has adverse implications for political participation of various kinds. Then I evaluate the extent to which these two proposed processes of influence – intrapersonal ambivalence and interpersonal social accountability – account for the overall impact of the network on political participation.

To investigate these questions, I have drawn on representative national surveys that tapped characteristics of respondents' political discussion networks as well as political participation. These included the Spencer survey and the American component of the Cross-National Election Project.[57]

It should be noted that the measures I draw on are very different from what has typically been used in the original studies of cross-pressures. In the original studies, group memberships were used as the basis for inferring that cross-cutting contact had occurred. But it is a huge leap from knowing that a person is both Catholic and a businessperson, for example, to inferring that he or she is therefore subject to political

[57] Details on the wording of individual survey items used in this chapter and on the coding of all measures can be found in Mutz (2002a). For details on CNEP data collection, see Beck, Dalton, & Huckfeldt (1995).

cross-pressures from pro-Democratic Catholic acquaintances and pro-Republican businesspeople. It is far less of a leap when that same person names the members of those groups as part of his or her immediate network. But even knowing the political characteristics of those in one's network does not ensure that cross-cutting exposure has occurred. For this reason, the measures used in this chapter also take into account the frequency of political discussion with each discussant. Even if one's network includes people who have oppositional political viewpoints, it is difficult to argue that cross-pressures are at work if political views are never communicated.

The two surveys complemented one another well for these purposes. The Spencer survey provided extensive information on exposure to oppositional political views and some variables useful for pinning down mechanisms of influence, while providing more limited information on political participation. The CNEP study, in contrast, included more participation measures plus a question addressing time of presidential vote decision, but it incorporated less information on exposure to political difference within the respondent's network. Unquestionably, both surveys represent an improvement over simply assuming cross-cutting exposure on the basis of membership in combinations of particular religious, economic, occupational, age, or racial categories that may (or may not) be central to an individual's social network; that may (or may not) represent oppositional political perspectives; and that may (or may not) exert cross-pressures on respondents through political communication.[58]

---

[58] In general, the extent of accuracy in respondents' self-reports on the political leanings of political discussants is relatively high, see, e.g., Huckfeldt & Sprague (1995a). Moreover, because the CNEP data included independent reports of candidate choice by the discussants themselves, the extent of projection in respondents' perceptions is known. Only 12% of the respondent–discussant dyads showed potential evidence of projection of the respondents' political views onto the discussant, and a full 78% of respondents' perceptions were accurate reports of the discussants' views; the remaining 9% were situations in which perceptual errors were made in the direction of a candidate *other* than the respondent's favored one (Mutz & Martin 2001). Only 8% of dyads involved perceptual errors in which the respondent preferred one candidate and erroneously claimed that the discussant preferred the same one. The remaining 4% (of the 12% mentioned) were cases in which a neutral discussant was erroneously perceived to favor the respondent's own candidate.

Despite high levels of accuracy in respondent perceptions, some might consider the discussants' reports superior to those provided by the respondents. However, for

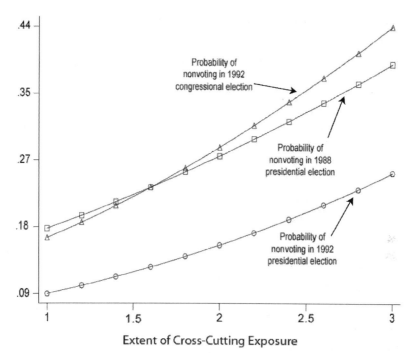

FIGURE 4.2. Effects of network composition on nonvoting in presidential and congressional elections. (Note: For full equations used to produce this figure, see Mutz 2002, table 1, columns 1 and 2. The vertical axis represents predicted probabilities based on logit equations setting all other variables at their means.)

Figure 4.2 summarizes the strength of the relationship between cross-cutting exposure and the likelihood of voting in presidential and congressional elections, *after* controlling for political interest, strength of partisanship (both Democratic and Republican), education, income, age, sex, frequency of political talk, and size of the person's political discussion network.[59] In these data the likelihood of voting is a function of the usual predictors such as high levels of political interest, strong

purposes of operationalizing social influences on the respondent, it makes little sense to argue that discussants' views will influence the respondent even when these views have not been clearly communicated. Although the choice of measure makes no real difference in these particular data, arguing that respondents will experience cross-pressures to the extent that they *recognize* that their network members hold differing political views makes more theoretical sense.

[59] For full details on the findings illustrated in this figure as well as in all subsequent ones in this chapter, please consult Mutz (2002a).

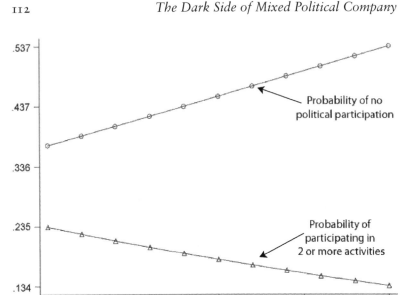

Extent of Cross-Cutting Exposure

FIGURE 4.3. Effects of network composition on extent of political activity. (Note: Findings shown are based on the analyses in Mutz 2002, table 1, column 3. The vertical axis represents predicted probabilities based on logit equations, setting all other variables at their means.)

partisanship, education, and the frequency of political discussion. But as shown in Figure 4.2, there is also a sizable and significant negative influence that stems from the extent of cross-cutting exposure in one's personal network. Having friends and associates of opposing political views makes it less likely that a person will vote. This relationship is particularly pronounced for nonvoting in congressional elections, although it also applies to nonvoting in the presidential context. The greater the cross-cutting exposure in the person's network, the more likely he or she is to abstain from voting.

Cross-cutting exposure also demonstrated a negative influence on an index of six participation items similar to the American National Election Studies participation battery. Not surprisingly, a high frequency of talk and large network size encourage recruitment into activities such as donating money to candidates and putting up signs. But here again, as shown in Figure 4.3, cross-cutting exposure is negatively related to participation. The probability that an individual will report not

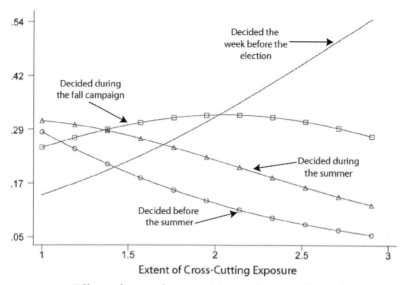

FIGURE 4.4. Effects of network composition on lateness of presidential vote decision. (Note: Findings shown are based on the analyses in Mutz 2002, table 1, column 4. The vertical axis represents predicted probabilities based on logit equations, setting all other variables at their means.)

participating in any of these activities steadily increases with higher levels of cross-cutting exposure; in contrast, the likelihood of participating in two or more activities steadily declines. Political activists are likely to inhabit an information environment full of like-minded others who spur them on to additional political activity.

Yet another way in which cross-pressures have been argued to reduce political participation is by promoting political decisions that are made later in the campaign season. If people make up their minds late in an election year, then there is little time or opportunity for actively partisan forms of political participation. In Figure 4.4, I illustrate the effects of network composition on the timing of presidential voting decisions. Although this figure looks a bit more complicated, it tells essentially the same story: Exposure to dissonant views encourages people to make up their minds later in the campaign, thus discouraging partisan forms of participation. As illustrated, the probability of deciding only the week before the election increases dramatically with greater cross-cutting exposure in a person's network. The likelihood of deciding on a presidential candidate early, say, before or during the

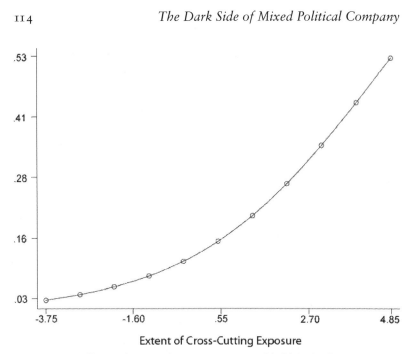

FIGURE 4.5. Effects of network composition on likelihood of reporting no intent to vote in the 1996 presidential election. (Note: Findings shown are based on the analyses in Mutz 2002, table 1, column 5. The vertical axis represents predicted probabilities based on logit equations, setting all other variables at their means.)

summer, declines with more heterogeneous networks. Although this measure does not directly tap participation, it seems inevitable that the later one makes up his or her mind, the less time there is for actively promoting one's political preferences.

In Figure 4.5 I draw on a completely different national survey and find that *intent to vote* in a preelection survey – this time in the 1996 presidential election – is also negatively influenced by cross-cutting exposure. Even employing the more stringent controls included in this survey (political knowledge in addition to political interest), cross-cutting exposure encourages respondents to report no intent to vote.

Drawing on every available indicator of political participation across these two surveys, my findings are extremely consistent: cross-cutting exposure discourages political participation. This pattern of findings is extremely robust even when using two different surveys with slightly different ways of tapping network composition and participation. Nonetheless, given that these are cross-sectional surveys, it is important to acknowledge the possibility that causality might run in the reverse direction. In other words, is it plausible that participating in political activities could *lead* one to associate with a more politically homogeneous group of contacts? If so, political participation could be causing lower levels of cross-cutting exposure rather than the other way around. If we call to mind highly social participatory acts such as working on a campaign or attending a fundraiser, it is relatively easy to entertain this possibility; through these kinds of events, one would make more like-minded friends and acquaintances. But for the remaining, equally supportive results, reverse causation makes no theoretical sense. The act of voting or of making up one's mind does not require a person to be in a particular social environment that is more conducive to like-minded views. Thus the bulk of evidence so far supports the idea that the degree of supportiveness of people's social environments influences their likelihood of political participation.

But it is also important to consider the possibility that some other factor could be simultaneously affecting levels of cross-cutting exposure and the extent of participation, thus making it appear as if they are causing one another. For example, those who have high levels of political interest and/or strongly partisan views might, as a result, be more likely to participate *and* be more likely to actively construct politically congenial social networks. Thus networks involving disagreement would go hand in hand with lower levels of participation, but not because cross-cutting exposure was *causing* people to refrain from political activity.

To what extent should we question the findings on these grounds? In the analyses described, controls are included for political interest, strength of partisanship, and, with the Spencer data, for political knowledge as well. And most of the other likely suspects work against such a relationship. For example, being a member of the workforce makes it more likely that a person will be politically active,[60] but because it also exposes people to many cross-cutting political

[60] Verba, Schlozman, & Brady (1995).

discussions,[61] it should produce a positive, rather than a negative, spurious association.

But *Why* Do Cross-Pressures Matter?

Unfortunately this highly consistent pattern of findings, in itself, tells us little about the nature of the social psychological processes underlying this effect. As a result, it does little to help cross-pressures attain status as a genuine "theory" of political behavior. How can we tell whether it is ambivalence driving people's avoidance of politics or a desire to maintain smooth social relationships with others? To examine the role of ambivalence, I created measures that simultaneously take into account both the respondent's overall intensity of feelings toward the candidates and the extent to which people's attitudes toward the candidates differ from one candidate to the next. So, for example, a person who had identically strong negative (or positive) feelings toward two candidates would be considered highly ambivalent. A person who had strong negative feelings toward one candidate and strong positive ones toward the other would have the lowest possible ambivalence score; if such a person wanted to vote, the decision would be easy. A person who evaluated the two candidates identically, but relatively neutrally, would be considered less ambivalent than a person who evaluated the two candidates identically but had stronger attitudes toward both.[62]

One way to get a sense of the relative contributions made by ambivalence and social accountability is to introduce this measure of ambivalence into the analysis and observe the extent to which it accounts for the effects of cross-cutting exposure. If ambivalence accounts for all of the effects of cross-cutting exposure, then we would conclude that ambivalence is primarily responsible for the effects observed thus far, and cross-cutting exposure is only important insofar as it encourages ambivalence.

This analysis was accomplished by including ambivalence in people's choice of a presidential candidate when predicting how likely it is that they would vote in the 1992 presidential election. As predicted, ambivalence toward the two candidates is a strong and significant

---

[61] Mutz & Mondak (1998).
[62] See Thompson, Zanna, & Griffin (1995); also see Breckler (1994).

predictor of abstention from voting in the presidential election. But quite surprisingly, cross-cutting exposure is just as strong a predictor of nonvoting as it was back in Figure 4.2; in fact, the results were virtually identical.

This pattern is very puzzling. People who are ambivalent about the candidates are naturally less enthusiastic about voting. This makes perfect sense. But ambivalence does little to explain why cross-cutting exposure dampens people's enthusiasm for political participation.

The pattern also provides evidence, albeit indirect, that social accountability is probably at work as well as ambivalence in translating cross-cutting exposure to political inaction. The inclusion of ambivalence as an additional control variable does not eradicate the effects of cross-cutting exposure, and this means that social accountability probably explains a great deal. However, subtractive logic is a weak basis on which to build a case for the idea that social accountability hampers participation (i.e., if it is not ambivalence, then it must be accountability). I attempted to construct a more direct test of the social accountability explanation by setting up two tests that ought to work *only* if social accountability is indeed a relevant factor in discouraging participation.

Fortunately, one of these two surveys included a psychological battery of items tapping people's reluctance to involve themselves in face-to-face conflict. If the social accountability explanation holds any water, then we would expect those who are conflict-avoidant to be particularly sensitive to cross-cutting exposure. Second, if both ambivalence and social accountability are taken into account in a single analysis, then one would expect to see the effects of cross-cutting exposure disappear entirely unless there is yet another mechanism at work that I have yet to identify.

The results in Figure 4.6 suggest that social accountability is extremely important to explaining this phenomenon. As expected, we see that cross-cutting exposure discourages participation strictly among those who avoid face-to-face conflict. Figure 4.6 provides a dramatic illustration of how people's desires to maintain interpersonal harmony lead them to abstain from political participation. The likelihood of nonvoting among those who do not particularly dislike face-to-face conflict is virtually unaffected by the extent of cross-cutting exposure in the social environment, as illustrated by the flat line in Figure 4.6.

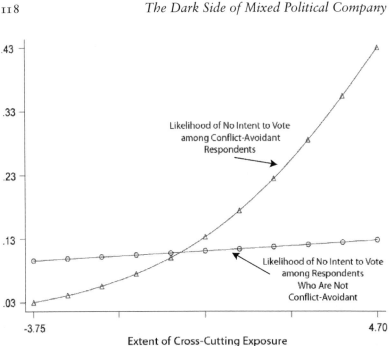

FIGURE 4.6. Effects of network composition on no intent to vote in presidential election, controlling for ambivalence, by individual differences in conflict avoidance. (Note: Findings shown are based on the analyses in Mutz 2002, table 5. The vertical axis represents predicted probabilities based on logit equations, setting all other variables at their means.)

Among the conflict-avoidant, in contrast, as people's social environments offer less support for their views, the likelihood that they will abstain from voting climbs quite steeply. Cross-cutting exposure clearly matters if you dislike conflict. For those who do not, it is irrelevant to their political participation. This pattern provides strong evidence that for many people avoiding political involvement is a means of avoiding interpersonal conflict and controversy.

But are there still other mechanisms at work that might explain the effects of cross-cutting exposure? When the analysis takes into account both ambivalence and social accountability, cross-cutting exposure no longer has any significant effects on participation. This finding suggests that collectively these two theories do a good job of accounting for the sum total of effects stemming from cross-cutting exposure.

Social Accountability in Public and Private Participation

In considering this collection of findings as a whole, one surprising pattern of results is that the size and strength of effects from cross-cutting exposure appear to be independent of whether the political act itself is private, as is the act of voting, as opposed to more public types of political acts. One would expect that social accountability would be relatively benign when considering private acts, but this does not appear to be the case in these results, nor in those of previous studies. Even though one could conceivably lie about whether and for whom one voted if asked, this privately executed behavior is still subject to social influences. Previous studies of the effects of social context on voting behavior have similarly suggested that social context influences both individual and social forms of participation. This may be because the events leading up to the participation are socially structured even when the act itself is performed in isolation.[63]

In addition, when one asks someone whether he or she voted, whether in surveys or in day to day life, this question is most often followed by the obvious question of *for whom* the person voted. If such a question is posed by a coworker or a survey interviewer, it is almost always followed by a question asking one to reveal one's preferences. If one is unsure of the other person's political leanings, then nonvoting is the safest answer. But even if the person being asked knows the other person's preferences, being cornered into a situation in which one is tempted to lie is stressful for most people, and thus it may be easier just to claim nonvoter status.

As expected, I found that cross-cutting exposure did, in fact, significantly influence levels of ambivalence in both of the surveys. Furthermore, ambivalence negatively influenced the likelihood of participation, just as predicted. But the explanation represented by the lower path in Figure 4.1 was far more important than anticipated. The social accountability explanation accounted for the majority of the influence from cross-cutting exposure.

Nonetheless, one additional finding suggests that perhaps the theoretical distinction between intrapersonal conflict–ambivalence (conflict within one's own thoughts and feelings) and interpersonal

[63] See Kenny (1992).

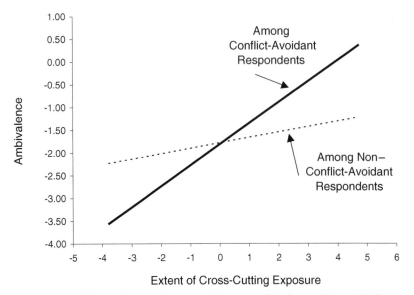

FIGURE 4.7. Effects of network composition on ambivalence. (Note: Findings shown are based on the analyses in Mutz 2002, table 1, columns 2 and 3. The vertical axis represents predicted values of ambivalence-based ordinary least squares equations, setting all other variables at their means.)

conflict–social accountability (conflict between one's own views and those of others) is mistaken in its compartmentalization of these two mechanisms of influence. As I have described, cross-cutting exposure significantly predicts ambivalence in both data sets. More surprising, however, is the fact that cross-cutting exposure's impact on ambivalence is *also* concentrated among the conflict-avoidant.

As shown in Figure 4.7, cross-cutting exposure encourages ambivalence particularly among those who are conflict-averse. Does it make sense that the effects of cross-cutting exposure on ambivalence are conditioned on aversion to conflict? Although my model has the intrapersonal–cognitive and interpersonal–social parts of this experience neatly compartmentalized, this is, not surprisingly, not how people live their lives. In fact, the evidence in Figure 4.7 is entirely consistent with recent laboratory evidence suggesting that conflicting influences within people's interpersonal networks can foster expressions of ambivalence even in the absence of new information that might produce internal conflict for an individual.[64] In this case, the cause of ambivalence is not the introduction of new or conflicting *information* that makes the political decision difficult. Instead, ambivalence is produced by discomfort with conflicts within the social environment.

Ultimately, then, the two processes of influence that I have outlined are tightly intertwined such that conflict aversion conditions people's reactions to cross-cutting exposure directly, by discouraging participation, and indirectly, by encouraging greater ambivalence. My results suggest that cross-cutting exposure's effects on expressions of ambivalence are primarily due to social concerns as well. I find no evidence supporting the idea that it is the *informational* influence of cross-cutting exposure that produces internally ambivalent citizens. It is possible, of course, that expressions of ambivalence constructed from survey responses do not accurately represent people's internal states. Such expressions are semiprivate at best, and thus they may incorporate some of the same social anxiety that leads cross-cutting networks to inhibit participation.

The consistency and robustness of these findings across data sets and across various participatory acts support the social psychological interpretation of these relationships as resulting from the social consequences of living in mixed political company. Moreover, because these models already take into account political interest, partisan extremity, and, in some cases, political knowledge, they may provide relatively conservative estimates of the total impact of cross-cutting exposure. For example, to the extent that cross-cutting exposure decreases participation indirectly by depressing political interest,[65] such effects would not be manifested in the strength of these relationships.

When drawing conclusions based on cross-sectional survey data it is always possible that some unidentified, unmeasured factor is producing misleading associations, in this case between cross-cutting exposure and political participation. Most of the plausible alternative explanations have been ruled out here. But even if one is not compelled by this evidence to believe that cross-cutting exposure dampens levels of participation, the fact that high levels of participation go hand in hand

[64] Priester & Petty (2001).
[65] See Funk (2001).

with homogeneous networks is still a substantively important finding for democratic theory. The association alone, without the causal icing on the cake, is cause for consternation. If political action is being carried out by those least well equipped with the kind of cross-cutting exposure that facilitates balanced judgments, then the quality of those decisions may suffer as a result. As shown in Chapter 3, exposure to those with views unlike one's own makes people more aware of legitimate rationales for opposing viewpoints and encourages greater tolerance, yet those who participate most have less exposure of this kind.

Cross-Pressures Resurrected

By moving closer to measuring the actual concept of interest in the theory of cross-pressures, scholars may ultimately revise the accepted conclusions about their impact. In this chapter, I have gone well beyond using paired group memberships that might logically be inferred to produce conflict through social interaction, and even beyond measures that consider the partisan composition of an individual's social network, to assess the extent of actual exposure to cross-cutting political communication within the network. Doing so appears to challenge the currently accepted consensus on whether cross-cutting social influences have implications for political participation. As in Chapter 3, further replications across more than the two data sets used here are obviously in order before reaching broader conclusions, but the consistency of these findings across different measures of participation and across data sets suggests that this line of inquiry may have been abandoned prematurely.

Interestingly, in response to an early draft of this chapter, I received a review indicating that although the findings themselves were compelling, these results were already well known and firmly established within political science, thus the paper was not worthy of publication except as a replication of previous work. These comments sent me scrambling back to the library to find the evidence I had missed. What I discovered instead was that the impression this reviewer had was born of the classic "file drawer" bias against null findings, and the tendency for findings from classic studies to take on a semipermanent life of their own. Although some null findings could be found here and there in published work, as null findings they were not the central focus of these publications, thus they attracted little attention. Moreover, many were published in sociology journals, where political scientists would be unlikely to notice them. The legacy of cross-pressures appears to have continued even if the evidence did not support it.

Perhaps more importantly, the contribution of this chapter goes beyond challenging the current consensus on *whether* cross-cutting networks have consequences to explain *why* they affect participation. The results in this chapter suggest that people entrenched in politically heterogeneous social networks retreat from political activity mainly out of a desire to avoid putting their social relationships at risk. This interpretation is supported by the fact that it is those who are conflict avoidant, in particular, who are most likely to respond negatively to cross-cutting exposure by limiting their political participation. Exposure to those with political views different from one's own also creates greater ambivalence about political options and thus makes decisive political action more difficult. But even expressions of ambivalence are themselves conditioned by a desire to avoid social conflict; cross-cutting exposure leads to ambivalence primarily among those who fear face-to-face conflict.

Tragedy or Triumph?

Although they are obviously linked in practice, the two processes of influence I have outlined typically differ in the kinds of normative implications that are drawn from them. Most would not chastise citizens for backing off from political participation because they are ambivalent toward candidates or policy positions. Few would blame citizens for their lack of decisiveness if it results from giving full consideration to a complex decision. This is, after all, the work of the diligent, deliberative citizen. If a person truly has no strong preference toward one political position or candidate because he or she finds it difficult to resolve the competing considerations weighing on various sides, then it would seem perverse to expect that person to be a political activist, and delaying political decisions would appear to be a logical and sensible response.

On the other hand, political withdrawal caused by a fear of the possible responses of others in one's social environment will strike most as more problematic in terms of what it says about American political culture. Likewise, ambivalence that results from external social pressure as opposed to competing internal considerations appears unhealthy for purposes of democratic decision making. Surely political disagreement is possible without risk of damage to one's interpersonal relationships. As mentioned in Chapter 2, some research suggests that conflict between one's own and others' views may be particularly difficult for Americans compared to citizens of other countries,[66] though relatively little is known about cross-cultural comparisons of the extent to which *political* disagreement is deemed socially acceptable.

But given that political activism in the contemporary United States *does* involve social risks, how harshly should we judge citizens for taking this potential cost into account? It is difficult to fault citizens for valuing smooth social interactions and wanting to get along with diverse others on a day to day basis. Because political interactions evoke anxieties and sometimes threaten social bonds, they are not always seen as an attractive prospect, particularly for those located in heterogeneous social environments.

The findings in this chapter could be viewed as tragic by those who think political participation is the ultimate measure of democratic performance. The meek and mild abstain from participation so as not to offend anyone, while ideologically extreme political bullies rule the Earth. Alternatively, it could be viewed as a triumph of pluralist politics. Americans have evolved a means of maintaining social harmony across lines of political difference by relegating their desires to have their own way, and their right to speak their own minds, to secondary status. In Chapter 5 I explore the implications of both perspectives, and ways they might be incorporated into theoretical frameworks that value both deliberative and participatory democracy.

---

[66] See Peng & Nisbett (1999).

5

The Social Citizen

If it were possible to control the characteristics of people's social environments in order to maximize democratic ends, what kind of political network would we ideally want them to have? Should the people in it be politically like-minded or have opposing political views? Those who are quick to jump to the conclusion that this network should be one that exposes people to as many oppositional political views as possible need to consider the quandary posed by the findings in Chapters 3 and 4: the kind of network that encourages an open and tolerant society is not necessarily the same kind that produces an enthusiastically participative citizenry. To be sure, some individual characteristics, such as levels of education and political knowledge, have uniformly positive implications for what is generally valued in democratic citizens. But the political diversity of people's face-to-face networks is unfortunately not one of these.

Political diversity poses a disturbing dilemma for images of the ideal citizen. There is a tendency to see the model citizen as a neat package of characteristics that all fit comfortably together into a single composite portrait. The problem is that for some very logical reasons these characteristics do not cohere. We want the democratic citizen to be enthusiastically politically active and strongly partisan, yet not to be surrounded by like-minded others. We want this citizen to be aware of all of the rationales for opposing sides of an issue, yet not to be paralyzed by all of this conflicting information and the cross-pressures it brings to bear. We want tight-knit, close networks of mutual trust, but we want them to be among people who frequently disagree. And we want frequent conversations involving political disagreement that have no repercussions for people's personal relationships. At the very least this is a difficult bill to fill.

I can offer no easy solution to this dilemma. No amount of torturing the data made it possible for me to explain away this contradiction, nor to contrive a reason why the practical impact of this contradiction should be benign. Nonetheless, if the nature of people's political networks involves important trade-offs, it seems incumbent upon political theorists to take this into account. How do we conceptualize a framework within which a diverse array of ordinary people can live their lives as both active citizens in a competitive political system and as compassionate fellow human brings? In particular, how do we accomplish this when one of these tasks appears to require strong partisanship and confident judgments about which political choices are right and which are wrong, while the other requires a tolerant, open-minded, nonjudgmental nature, and an acceptance of people's worth on their own terms, however disagreeable we may find their political views?

There are, of course, times and places in which this determination is not so difficult. When politics becomes extreme enough or so clear-cut that even the most timid are enjoined to take sides, then it is easy to see the good citizen and the good human being as one and the same in their actions. But what is surprising in the United States, given our general lack of politically extreme groups, is just how difficult people nonetheless find it to negotiate their political and apolitical identities. When they are among like-minded others, this is not a problem. But in the company of strangers or those known to be of oppositional views, people find this quite difficult. A highly politicized mindset of "us" versus "them" is easy so long as we do not work with "them" and our kids do not play with their kids. But how do we maintain this same fervor and political drive against "them" when we carpool together?

For the most part, I think we do this by downgrading the importance of politics in our everyday lives. We reconcile these identities by pointing out that politics is merely one of many different dimensions of who we are as human beings. We avoid head-to-head political discussions in order to maintain the kind of social harmony that we also value. We implicitly, nonconsciously choose a point along a scale forcing a trade-off between a strong political identity that silently (or not so silently) disparages those of opposing views and a more politically diverse social life that is made possible (in part) by its apolitical nature. Those whose identities are more explicitly political will tend to attract and seek out those of like mind. And this camaraderie will further encourage the kind of activism valued by enthusiasts of participatory democracy. Those who do not wear their politics on their sleeves will have more opportunities to hear the other side from others in their environments. But those mixed allegiances, cross-pressures, and (most likely) moderate political positions will come with a reduced likelihood of political activism. The voice of moderation is seldom very loud. And it is difficult, perhaps impossible, to foment political fervor over middle-of-the-road views. Further, although successful deliberation may elicit compromises, these will seldom elicit the cheers and enthusiasm that go along with "beating" the other side.

People within homogeneous networks encourage and reinforce one another in their viewpoints, and this tendency makes activism and fomenting of fervor far easier. Like-minded social environments are ideal for purposes of encouraging political mobilization. "Enclave deliberation," that is, conversation among like-minded people, promotes recognition of common problems and helps individuals spur one another on to collective action.[1] For this reason, participation and involvement are best encouraged by social networks that offer reinforcement and encouragement, not networks that demand compromise or that raise the social costs of political engagement. Paradoxically, the prospects for deliberative democracy could be dwindling at the same time that prospects for participation and political activism are escalating.

Normative Implications for Partisanship

The discussions of political agreement and disagreement throughout this book have not explicitly addressed the question of agreement or

---

[1] See Sunstein (2002) for a discussion. Of course, some theorists might not consider it "deliberation" at all because of the absence of oppositional viewpoints (e.g., Gutmann & Thompson [1996]).

disagreement with respect to what? In part this is because regardless of whether I used measures of the extent to which respondents and discussants were of the same party, whether they voted for the same candidates, or whether they simply reported a great deal of agreement in their political conversations, the responses were very strongly related and thus seemed indicative of a single underlying concept.

But undoubtedly, the main organizing construct for political agreement and disagreement in the United States, the most visible form of political categorization, lies in the two political parties. Even though most Republicans and Democrats seldom, if ever, meet as a political group, these identities tend to persist thoughout the lifetime and to have a strong influence on political behavior.[2] If partisanship is the central organizing principle for agreement and disagreement in Americans' social interactions, then these findings also have implications for the normative value of partisan identities for voters.

Although scholars have addressed the question of whether political parties are good for the political system, few have evaluated this same question at the level of the individual citizen: Are Americans better citizens when they adopt partisan identities? Implicit in this book's evidence is an argument for promoting partisanship, as well as one for discouraging it. In the first case, partisan labels and self-identification facilitate like-minded interactions, which are important for purposes of uniting people around common political causes and a shared purpose and for orienting them to take collective action. But in the second case, partisan identities are also known to hinder information processing: "Partisanship appears to reflect bias, thoughtlessness, cowardice of mind, asocial contentiousness and faltering devotion to the common good."[3] In this respect, partisanship is the antithesis of open-mindedness and tolerance. Partisans have already decided who is right and who is wrong, and thus they are unlikely to be objective judges of political information. Instead, their perceptual biases reinforce and perpetuate strong differences of opinion between Republicans and Democrats.[4]

---

[2] See Green, Palmquist, & Schickler (2002) for the most recent treatment of the influence of partisanship.

[3] Muirhead (2005, p. 2).

[4] The original source of this observation is the Berelson, Lazarsfeld, & McPhee (1954) landmark *Voting*, and it was further reinforced by Campbell, Converse, Miller, &

For these reasons, political theory has often treated partisanship as normatively undesirable.[5] Many members of the American public apparently feel the same way, and thus they shun partisan labels.[6] In an era of intense concern over "red" versus "blue" America and "culture wars," it is easy to see why partisanship has acquired a bad name, at least in the eyes of apolitical observers. But curiously, even strong partisans often see partisanship as unnecessary. As Muirhead notes:

Partisans have a certain distaste for partisanship, at least if it is to include the partisanship of those they oppose. And they do not tend to perceive their own side as very partisan at all, since it seems defensible to them. To the Democratic eye, Republicans appear heartless and mean. Republicans experience Democrats as irresponsibly innocent. Depending on where one stands, one's opponents lack either intelligence or compassion, and in either case the partisanship of the other side seems to reflect something more defective in it than in oneself. Perhaps this defect is something we can understand. Or perhaps it reveals something worse, something negligent – even evil. In either case, one's own partisanship seems, simply, right, one's opponents' wrong.[7]

Interestingly, this portrayal of partisanship – as more or less an affliction – is in stark contrast to its characterization in empirical studies of American political behavior. In studies of mass behavior, partisans are typically the "good guys." They are the ones who always score highest on political knowledge tests, who vote most frequently, volunteer their time and money for campaigns, and basically embody everything that social scientists say they want *all* citizens to be. Or do we? When partisanship is cast as a form of prejudice, as a psychological blinder that impedes the individual's processing of political information, then its status as an individual trait becomes suspect.

But as the ancient Chinese proverb puts it, "The other side also has an other side." Although it may do little for enlarged sensibility or tolerance, partisanship can, nonetheless, be valued for its ability

Stokes (1960) *The American Voter*. This conclusion has been questioned in some more recent work on Bayesian learning, but analyses using panel data have ultimately reinforced the idea that Republicans and Democrats respond very differently to politically relevant events. See Bartels (2002) for details.

[5] Muirhead (2003).

[6] See Wattenberg (1994, p. 176).

[7] Muirhead (2005, p. 4).

to motivate and facilitate political action. In defense of partisanship, Muirhead argues that partisans

make elections happen (they vote, stuff envelopes, knock on doors, drive people to the polls, make phone calls, contribute money, design strategy, and run for office). They are the ones who cheer in joy and who mourn in sorrow on election night – and either way, steel themselves for another fight. If they are prejudiced, narrow and blind in some respects (and they are), they are also idealistic, inspired and knowing.[8]

According to this view, were it not for deep, fundamental political disagreements between partisans, it is unlikely that people would become as engaged as they are in the political process. If disagreements were at the level of technical details on how to implement consensus policies, matters of mere expertise rather than differences in core values, then it is unlikely that passionate partisanship would survive. It is this kind of passion, and this high level of confidence in one's own views, that drives political participation. If a given person lacks complete faith in the grounding of his or her political convictions, then why would he or she devote time and money to proselytizing for one outcome over another?

Muirhead's defense of passionate partisanship parallels Michael Schudson's argument about how progressive era electoral reforms robbed American politics of much of its passion, and thus also sapped a good deal of the public's motivation for mass participation. When progressive reforms promoted the notion of educational citizenship, of "perusing, not parading,"[9] individual consumption of political information substituted for crowds, celebrations, and torchlight parades.

But the defense of partisanship as more than just another form of prejudice or narrowmindedness extends beyond the value of passion as a motivator of political participation. Drawing on John Stuart Mill, a great advocate of partisanship and himself a strong partisan, Muirhead suggests that "we are unlikely to form any comprehensive understanding of political things if we bypass the partisan's stand. It is as if in order to see anything and to stand for anything, we need to give ourselves over to a particular and partial perspective."[10] It is for this reason that

---

[8] Muirhead (2005, p. 2).
[9] Schudson (1992, p. 158).
[10] Muirhead (2003, p. 18) draws on Mill's discussion in "Bentham" (1969).

Mill urges "a large tolerance for one-eyed men, provided their eye is a penetrating one: if they saw more, they probably would not see so keenly, nor so eagerly pursue one course of enquiry."[11]

According to Muirhead, Mill suggested that these two different kinds of citizens – impassioned partisans and disinterested observers – both serve important purposes in the political world. Partisans provide a partial, but deep understanding of the political world and the convictions and passion to promote their views. One assumes that these citizens inhabit largely like-minded enclaves of political deliberation, and that these experiences help to deepen their own understandings. The disinterested observers provide a measure of tolerance born of indifference, but they also play an important role in the political process by virtue of their open-mindedness. Mill recognized that partisans were unlikely to be persuaded by the views of opposing partisans. Instead, the "combatants fighting" are for the benefit of the disinterested observers. As he put it, "It is not on the impassioned partisan, it is on the calmer and more disinterested bystander, that this collision of opinion works its salutary effect."[12]

The problem with much of what deliberative democracy asks of participatory democrats is that both of these tasks – activism and deliberation – have been embedded in a single model as simultaneous responsibilities of the individual. For example, Muirhead suggests it is inaccurate to separate the impassioned partisans and the disinterested observers as Mill does. Instead, a given person must serve as both partisan and disinterested observer: "One part of us gives ourselves over to what we intuit, feel, and know – which gives rise to our particular perspective on things. But the giving over might be less than complete, thus preserving an observing self that looks at our own commitment from a distance."[13] While this is an extremely attractive possibility in theory, I am skeptical that it could ever occur on a meaningful scale. The detached perspective on one's own views is certainly possible, but its likelihood varies in inverse proportion to the extent of participation. It is important for citizens to have an understanding of the other side, to be aware of legitimate rationales for views other than

---

[11] Mill (1969, p. 94).
[12] Mill (1956, p. 53) as cited in Muirhead (2003).
[13] Muirhead (2003, p. 19).

their own. But is it realistic to expect activists to continually reconsider their preferences?

A Delicate Balance?

This book is not the first to note a tension between participation and some other highly valued democratic outcome such as political tolerance, or acceptance of the legitimacy of oppositional views. In their five-country comparison featured in *The Civic Culture*, Almond and Verba were among the first to advance the idea that a "mixed" political culture would result in greater political stability than one with maximal levels of participation. By "mixed," Almond and Verba meant that a stable democracy involved trade-offs or "balanced disparities"[14] and blended contradictory goals such as consensus and cleavage. A completely activist political culture was no more desirable than a completely passive one, in their view, and democracy was said to be in balance only "when the heat of political conflict does not exceed or fall below a given temperature range."[15]

The Civic Culture presented the ideal political environment as one characterized by relatively high levels of tolerance as well as of participation, and one in which people talked frequently and openly about politics. In this sense it incorporated elements of deliberative democratic theory and theories of participatory democracy. Some citizens were supposed to be emotionally involved in elections, but certainly not all. And some were assumed to put the collective good ahead of their immediate, parochial interests at times, but not everyone, nor all the time.

The complementary roles assigned to politically active and passive citizens in this theory were seen by some as contrived claims for Anglo-American superiority. Of the five countries studied, Great Britain and the United States may not have had the highest rates of participation, for example, but they emerged as the most "balanced" political cultures, and this trait was asserted to account for their greater stability as democracies.

Few studies since have suggested that less than full participation might be acceptable or even desirable for democracies. One recent

---

[14] Almond (1995) cites Harry Eckstein as the source of this phrase.
[15] Almond (1995, p. 5).

exception is Franklin's "electoral competition model," which similarly acknowledges that high turnout is not necessarily a sign of a democracy's health and well-being;[16] likewise, low turnout does not necessarily indicate anything negative about the way citizens approach politics. According to his argument, low turnout says more about the nature of the country's electoral system and its level of competitiveness than it does about the civic virtue of its citizens.

The findings in this book suggest a trade-off with an ideal point that is unclear. Because both participation and tolerance are highly valued in democratic systems, there is no easy answer to the question of how much political inactivity should be accepted in the name of greater tolerance, nor, conversely, of how much intolerance of oppositional views should be accepted in the name of encouraging political activism. My results suggest that within any given individual, enthusiastic participation rarely coexists with ongoing exposure to diverse political viewpoints and careful consideration of the political alternatives. Deliberation and participation, in other words, do not go hand in hand. Homogeneous and heterogeneous social contexts serve two different, yet important, purposes in this regard.

As historical events illustrate, it would be overly simplistic and shortsighted to claim that democracy is best served by strictly heterogeneous or homogeneous networks. Homogeneous networks are not simply enclaves where people feel comfortable talking; they also play distinct, beneficial roles in the political world. For one, within the safety of like-minded settings, people who would not otherwise speak up may be heard.[17] Some demographic groups routinely remain quiet because of the risks involved in heterogeneous deliberative bodies. Without enclave deliberation, they would otherwise be "invisible, silenced or squelched."[18] The antislavery movement in the United States is just one example of a like-minded network that produced extremely valuable forms of political action.[19] Were it not for regular interactions among those of like mind, it is difficult to imagine social movements such as abolitionism or the gay rights movement.[20] Then again, Weimar

---

[16] Franklin (2004).

[17] Sunstein (2000).

[18] Sunstein (2002, p. 190) also points to the discussion of consciousness raising in MacKinnon (1989, pp. 83–105) as an example.

[19] Sunstein (2000) provides this as an example of the benefits of enclave deliberation.

[20] Ibid.

Germany is also an example of how homogeneous networks facilitate political participation, in this case along with obvious sacrifices in political tolerance. A proliferation of groups and associations involving dense networks mobilized German citizens for political action and simultaneously deepened cleavages among them.[21] It was from these highly homogeneous, highly activist groups that Hitler drew his most enthusiastic support.

And although polarization is generally considered a negative, advocates of "cool democracy" such as Almond and Verba acknowledge that in some cases the polarizing as well as the mobilizing characteristics of homogeneous networks may serve useful purposes by encouraging citizens to have more intense views.[22] Strongly held positions are generally a prerequisite for being willing to disturb political stability. And extremist sentiments have fueled many an important social movement. A civic culture would "run cool and avoid intense and sustained conflict and breakdown," but as a consequence of this balance, "it also meant the postponement and moderation of political action intended to achieve social justice."[23]

Of course, when political participation takes highly undesirable forms, siding with the advocates of heterogeneous political networks is easy. Cross-cutting social networks are known to decrease the likelihood of the kind of intergroup polarization that can lead to political violence.[24] But as we have seen, heterogeneous social contacts also subdue enthusiasm for more conventional and desirable forms of participation.

Thus homogeneity within a political network is not always a negative influence, but neither is it consistently beneficial to the success of any given social movement. Jane Mansbridge's fascinating history of the campaign to ratify the Equal Rights Amendment (ERA) illustrates the pitfalls inherent in ideologically driven political activism.[25] Because those active in the ERA movement could expect few instrumental benefits from their participation, they became involved as unpaid volunteers mainly because they were strongly committed to the principle. As "true

---

[21] Berman (1997).
[22] Almond & Verba (1989b).
[23] Almond (1995).
[24] See, e.g., Hewstone & Cairns (2001); Jalali & Lipset (1992/1993).
[25] Mansbridge (1986).

believers," they also tended to be more extreme in their portrayal of the changes that would result from ERA ratification. These more extreme interpretations, and the linking of the ERA with far more controversial issues such as abortion rights, participation of women in combat, and unisex bathrooms, ultimately made the proposed amendment far less popular than it was when the campaign for ratification began. On the one hand, caring deeply about a cause may seem the most noble motivation for political activism; on the other hand, self-selected activists may undermine the very efforts they seek to achieve through extreme and uncompromising rhetoric.

In short, political talk within homogeneous environments is both necessary at some times and dangerous at others. Conversations among the like-minded can be the engine for progressive change, drawing in those who rarely speak up politically and are seldom heard, but it can also be a force for destructive intolerance. What can be said unequivocally is that like-minded political interactions are useful for purposes of promoting political action. Whether that political action is harmful or beneficial in any given situation remains another question entirely.

Contradictions of Participatory Democracy

The contradictions inherent in an extremely activist political culture seem most obvious when we consider some of the key tenets of theories of participatory democracy. Theories of participatory democracy suggest that if you build it, they will come. In other words, if only governments would provide *meaningful* opportunities for people to participate in the political process, then citizens would be emboldened by their power and rise to these participatory occasions. The kinds of meaningful opportunities most often suggested by leading advocates include more direct referenda at the national level and greater citizen involvement in community-level political institutions.[26]

But if we build it *who* will come? When new or revitalized avenues for citizen participation are put into place, who is most likely to use them? Unfortunately, everything we know suggests that the people most likely to take advantage of increasing opportunities to participate in politics will tend to be systematically more extreme in their

[26] Barber (1984); Pateman (1970).

views and thus unrepresentative of the general population.[27] Just as Mansbridge observed in her study of ERA advocates, Fiorina likewise has noted that "the kinds of demands on time and energy required to participate politically are sufficiently severe that those willing to pay the costs come disproportionately from the ranks of those with intensely held, extreme views."[28] More participation would be fine if it involved everyone or even a representative subsample, but more participation primarily by those who have the most extreme and strongly held views could do more damage than good. Thus the problem with a highly politicized society is not strictly that the conditions necessary to produce it would damage other democratic values, though this also appears to be true. As Fiorina points out, the participation itself could also be detrimental to the extent that extremists prolong conflicts and prevent compromise.

By 2005, there was already mounting concern surrounding polarization in the American public. Some saw it occurring exclusively among political elites; others saw it growing in the mass public as well.[29] In the aftermath of a presidential election with the highest turnout in many years, the hand-wringing shifted from being about low turnout to a focus on excessive partisanship and polarization. Fiorina suggests that as increasing opportunities for participation have evolved over the last 50 years, politically active people have self-selected into progressively more extreme camps. Whether this pattern occurs because homogeneous networks foster greater extremism or because the more extreme self-select into more homogeneous environments remains to be seen. But in either case, the dilemma remains: how do we reconcile the demands of deliberative and participative democracy?

Unnatural Acts: The Social Psychology of Participation

Political communication of the face-to-face variety is among the most difficult forms of social interaction to negotiate. As Warren notes,

---

[27] Fiorina's (1999) case study of local politics over land use in Concord, Massachusetts, provides one illustration of how deliberation leads to more extreme participants in the decision-making process.

[28] Fiorina (1999, p. 416).

[29] For a series of newspaper articles on balkanization and concerns surrounding polarization trends in the United States, see www.Statesman.com/greatdivide

"Even under the best of circumstances, political relationships are among the most difficult of social relationships."[30] And talking about politics is not easy for many people across a broad variety of social contexts.[31]

Unfortunately, the way empirical scholars have tended to write about interpersonal political communication has drained it of much of its passion and social psychological tension. Instead, we describe face-to-face communication as being about information transmission, opinion leadership, or about conveying an agenda of issue importance, rather than about the social psychological nature of affiliation and differentiation. These commonly studied effects of face-to-face contact can and do happen, and they are not unimportant. But from a social psychological standpoint, the more interesting aspect of face-to-face communication about politics is the way it is safely integrated into the fabric of everyday lives and relationships.

Advocates of both deliberative and participatory democracy tend to gloss over these potentially unattractive features of their respective theories.[32] And yet as Warren suggests, for most Americans, "fitting in" typically means being apolitical: "Most people like to get along, identify with one another, be recognized and belong. Most of our day-to-day interactions reflect this: we don't (usually) go around with an 'attitude.'"[33] To be sure, there are times and places set aside for political discussion, but as discussed in Chapter 2, these account for very little of the total amount of political discussion that transpires in the United States, and they are subject to the same self-selection processes as are other forms of participation.

Theoretically, there are several ways that Americans could cope with the contradictions of good citizenship. The first, as previously noted, is simply to devalue politics. As Warren suggests, when one chooses to be a political person, the benefits must outweigh the costs of disrupting social relationships in order for the choice to be worth the price. If the

---

[30] Warren (1996, p. 244).

[31] Schudson (1997) elaborates on this theme, suggesting that sociable conversations should be differentiated from problem-solving conversations in determining the importance of political conversation to democracy.

[32] Warren (1996) proffers a similar critique of theories of participatory democracy in his essay, "What Should We Expect from More Democracy?"

[33] Ibid., pp. 251–252.

benefits do not reach this level, then it makes more sense to back off from a given controversy.

A second popular solution to this situation is to ensure that your political conversations are among like-minded others. Perhaps this is why Americans are so proficient at exercising their life choices so that they maintain networks largely devoid of political heterogeneity. When one is among friends of like mind, politics is no longer perilous territory.

Not surprisingly, most observers of American political culture find neither of these solutions acceptable. Devaluing politics is unacceptable, but so is political balkanization. There is, however, a third option for resolving the tension between deliberative and participatory ideals, besides devaluing politics or seeking politically like-minded environments. One could simply devalue social relationships and social harmony. So long as people do not care about offending others or provoking heated discussions in their social environments, or about differentiating and potentially distancing themselves from others, then passionate political participation can thrive even in mixed company. Interestingly, this option is seldom advocated by citizens or scholars, probably because it is dismissed as unrealistic. It is testimony to how much social relationships are valued over political ones that this alternative is not even considered. Instead, citizens are encouraged to value "community" and get along with their neighbors. "Putting our differences aside" translates to either avoiding politics or having like-minded neighbors.[34]

Yet another possibility for merging the good citizen and good neighbor roles is also popular. The kind of apolitical civic engagement that transpires in most voluntary associations is perfect for those who want to avoid the uncomfortable nature of partisan politics, yet still think of themselves as "good citizens." A volunteer is the quintessential good citizen.[35] Perhaps this elevated status is related to the fact that voluntary associations embrace largely apolitical goals, such as improving the school playground, preventing hunger, or collecting winter coats for those less fortunate. Even though it is just as time-consuming,

---

[34] At the same time, our culture also demonstrates admiration for those willing to speak out and accept whatever consequences follow (Gandhi and the Reverend Martin Luther King Jr. come to mind).

[35] Eliasoph (1998, p. 25); see also Schudson (1997).

participation that is oriented toward uncontroversial ends tends to be more popular than participation in partisan political causes.[36] A volunteer for the League of Women Voters is entirely different in status from a volunteer for the National Organization for Women.

If a voluntary association pursues controversial political goals, then it will primarily involve people who self-select into the group on the basis of already shared political views.[37] In this way, the discomfort of cross-cutting exposure is again successfully evaded. To be clear, these examples of civic engagement are *all* obviously worthwhile activities, but they are not controversial political actions that produce winners and losers, nor do they involve the same potential social costs. And most importantly, they do little to advance the cause of hearing the other side.

Experiential Diversity

Diversity of all kinds is widely touted as a *public* goal in the contemporary United States. And yet people's *private* behaviors reveal relatively little desire to seek out the pragmatic experience of exposure to those of differing perspectives. Although cross-cutting contact is conceptually appealing as an idea, many people find it uncomfortable in practice. Studies of intergroup contact suggest that it is precisely this anxiety and discomfort that interfere with the potentially positive effects of cross-cutting contact.[38]

Another part of the problem is that it is unclear precisely what is being advocated under the banner of diversity. What social scientists typically call diversity relies heavily on aggregate-level characteristics. It is assumed, for example, that cities are preferable to suburbs for purposes of interracial contact because these geographic areas are more diverse in terms of the aggregate percentages of whites and nonwhites

---

[36] See Eliasoph (1998) for a discussion of how voluntary association members talk about political topics.

[37] Popielarz & McPherson (1995); McPherson, Popielarz, & Drobnic (1992).

[38] See Wright, Aron, McLaughlin-Volpe, & Ropp (1997) for a discussion of how anxiety impedes positive intergroup contact. These authors show that "extended group contact" from just knowing one's friends are friends with the target group can alleviate the anxiety related to face-to-face contact, yet still produce positive attitudinal effects.

living there. In reality, these aggregate statistics tell us very little about the extent of interracial contact that individuals experience in cities. As Calhoun suggests, cities have always been segregated along lines of class and ethnicity, but avoidance of direct interactions has become far easier than ever before:

Large scale has combined with urban sprawl and explicit development plans to allow much urban diversity to be masked. Elites are shielded from the poor, particularly, but a variety of middle and working class groups are able to go about their urban lives in an almost complete lack of urbane contact with and awareness of each other.[39]

Despite high levels of diversity by aggregate standards, cities may nonetheless result in few everyday opportunities for residents to hear the other side. The extent of between-group diversity within an aggregate (the percentage of blacks versus whites versus other racial groups, or Republicans versus Democrats, for example) tells us very little about patterns of association within the aggregate. For example, a county evenly split between Republicans and Democrats, the oft-cited 50–50 America, would receive a maximal diversity score based on most methods of quantifying diversity. Consider two different scenarios: (1) a 50–50 community in which all Republicans live and work north of Main Street and all Democrats south of it, with each speaking to no one but like-minded partisans, or (2) a 50–50 community in which homes alternated between Republican and Democratic families, and cross-cutting conversations among friends and acquaintances were the norm. These two fictitious communities are clearly quite different with respect to people's likelihood of hearing the other side. And yet most methods would assign the same level of "diversity" to both.

For example, segregation indexes – one of the most commonly used measures – tell us the percentage of people who would need to move from one county (or other unit) to another in order for every county to have the same distribution of partisanship as the nation as a whole. But they tell us little about how much cross-cutting communication actually occurs. The segregation index for the distribution of Republicans and Democrats in American counties has been slowly rising since the late 1970s and stood at 21.6 percent as of the 2004 presidential

---

[39] Calhoun (1988, p. 226).

election.[40] Unfortunately we lack the data we would need to establish a trend for the extent of cross-cutting contact. Interestingly, studies of interracial contact suggest that black–white contact tends to be greater at moderate levels of segregation than at either the low or high end of the segregation spectrum.[41]

Models of the network selection process tend to emphasize the probabilistic effects of the social context on network composition, as outlined in Chapter 2. But unless a given area is *overwhelmingly* dominated by one party, there are typically enough like-minded people for even those in the minority to find like-minded political company if they are so motivated.

Making Conversation Safe for Political Diversity

How can a political culture that depends on the notion of free and open debate realize the benefits of frank discussion if it is seen to be at odds with the achievement of community and the pursuit of social harmony? Conflict between one's own and others' views may be particularly difficult for Americans compared to citizens of other countries.[42] As seen in Chapter 2, Americans *are* unusually adept at avoiding cross-cutting political discussion. Israelis, on the other hand, have been asserted to "use political talk the way Americans use talk about sports: to create common ground, with political disagreement only adding to the entertainment value."[43] But the tensions involved in maintaining both the social and the political self are not peculiarly American. As illustrated by the election poster in Figure 5.1, political disagreement has the potential to strain social relationships in any context involving oppositional views. This poster, produced by the National Commission on Democracy in Sierra Leone, suggests that it does *not* go without saying that political differences can be maintained within

---

[40] See Cushing & Bishop (2004).

[41] Sigelman, Bledsoe, Welch, & Combs (1996) find this in the context of racial diversity.

[42] Peng & Nisbett (1999) analyze attitudes cross-culturally and suggest this conclusion, but they do not target *political* disagreement in particular.

[43] Wyatt & Liebes (1995, p. 21). See also Wyatt, Katz, Levinsohn, & Al-Haj (1996). Note that the World Values evidence in Chapter 2 confirms that Israel has the highest level of political discussion of all countries in the World Values Surveys, though there is no comparable evidence on the extent of disagreement in these conversations.

FIGURE 5.1. Poster from Sierra Leone election.

the context of social relationships. Instead, this idea must be actively promoted.

As illustrated by the findings in Chapter 3, civility in political interactions can go a long way toward enabling participants in informal cross-cutting talk to derive more benefits from these interactions. Even Emily Post, the doyenne of social etiquette, recognized that manners are about more than how people should behave at fancy dinner parties. In her words, "Manners are a sensitive awareness of the feelings of others. If you have that awareness, you have good manners, no matter what fork you use."[44] But political etiquette is not as simple as social etiquette because citizens must combine multiple goals: the maintenance

---

[44] Emily Post, "Such Is Life." Available at http://www.creativequotations.com/one/1214.htm.

of social networks (the traditional focus of etiquette practices) and active pursuit of some political end.

But the question implied by the Israeli example is still worth asking: is there any way to make talking politics more like talking sports, a topic more conducive to bonding than to differentiation? This question may sound odd given that characterizing politics as a "spectator sport" is typically a derogatory claim. When citizens are "mere spectators," this is assumed to be undesirable because they are not actual participants in the process. And yet, I think the sports analogy and the spectator role may be undervalued. Some of the most comfortable informal cross-cutting interactions I have witnessed – such as my father's with his dentist – have sounded a lot like pregame conversations between fans of opposing teams. They involve some good-natured, though barbed teasing and some laughter, as well as some substantive arguments. But there is no mistaking that these two people disagree.

At least since the reforms of the progressive era, American citizens have been encouraged to take their politics very seriously. A comparison of the 2004 presidential debates and the 2004 Superbowl makes it very clear that politics is treated as a more solemn and serious matter than sports in our culture, and perhaps rightfully so. But it is worth noting that the presidential debates had no entertaining halftime show, balloons, or fireworks, nor were people allowed to scream and yell enthusiastically for their "team." In American political life, expertise and factoids have been elevated over opinion and passion as what is seen as the "appropriate" currency for political communication.

The information-based model of politics implies that there are right answers to most political questions, if only one were adequately informed.[45] If people disagree, and thus root for different teams, it cannot be simply that one is an Eagles fan and the other a Patriots fan: one person must be right, and the other wrong. As I watched the enforced stone silence of the audience for the debates (without beer or chips and dip by my side, I might add), it seemed entirely obvious to me why politics and religion are considered part of that same category of topics considered far too serious to discuss in mixed company. The debate setting might as well have been a church sanctuary in its silence, thus conveying the grave import of the event. By

---

[45] See Schudson (1998) for a full description of the informational model of citizenship.

ridding this political event of any Superbowl-like hoopla or enthusiasm, the format communicated to citizens that politics is really far too serious a form of disagreement among citizens to be aired out in the open as a sports rivalry might be. Of course, at national conventions of the like-minded, it is still considered acceptable to cheer for one's own team, but certainly not when both teams are in the same political stadium.

Conversation is about the search for similarity between people.[46] Anyone who has ever sat on an airplane beside a garrulous stranger recognizes the truth of this statement. "So, are you on business in Philly?" No, I live here. "Are you in sales?" Not exactly; I work for the University of Pennsylvania. "That must be a huge state school. I went to a big state school too." No, it's small and private. "Oh really. What kinds of things do you teach?" Political science. The passenger responds with relief: "Political science! I took a course in political science in college once." Yes, indeed, I reply; we must be first cousins.

This conversational exchange would sound inane were it not so commonplace. People involved in conversations naturally gravitate toward ideas or experiences that they have in common. Sometimes they initiate topic after topic after topic until they find conversational common ground. And they become still more engaged with one another as they find additional things in common – mutual friends, mutual interests, or mutual backgrounds. For this reason alone, it is questionable whether conversation is the best route to exposing people to oppositional political views.

But what are the alternatives? Political disagreement is particularly difficult to convey through conversation because of the tendency for people to assume agreement, especially when they like the other person. I see this tendency to assume unanimous agreement frequently in many social settings, including in academe, when political conversations begin with a statement that all but eliminates the possibility of hearing the other side. For example, the oft-quoted proclamation by liberals after the 2004 election that they were "moving to Canada" implied a lot more than the urge to move north. They may or may

---

[46] This observation was passed on to me by Neil Smelser, though he claims not to have been the source and was not aware of its origins.

not have been serious, but that is not the point.[47] Embedded in this assertion are two claims: (1) that all reasonable people must have supported the same presidential candidate that they did and (2) that one would naturally not want to live in an environment where people had political views different from one's own. Interestingly, the impetus for this statement was not a particular policy change in the United States that had instrumental effects on citizens – there was no time for that to have happened. Instead, it was a way of pointing out that they would be more comfortable living among Canadians who were of like mind, at least more so than the majority of Americans. Statements of this kind – and there are many varieties of them – not only do not encourage cross-cutting exposure, they practically forbid it.

Are There Plausible Alternatives?

Aside from avoiding conversation-stopping political rhetoric, what other possibilities exist for cross-cutting exposure? In recent years, some theorists have proposed that the future of communication across lines of political difference lies in technologies that transcend geographic space. As Calhoun argues, "In modern societies, most of the information we have about people different from ourselves comes not through any direct relationships, even the casual ones formed constantly in urban streets and shops. Rather it comes through print and electronic media."[48] Mediated exposure obviously differs in important ways from interpersonal contact, but it is conceivably another means by which people could hear the other side in an increasingly selection-driven social structure.

In the United States, the major problem with looking to news media to fulfill the need for cross-cutting political exposure is that the current trend in media industries is toward highly specialized rather than mass channels. As the number of potential places to obtain news multiplies, consumers must choose among them, and that exercise of choice may lead to less diversity of political exposure. Advertisers and

---

[47] See, e.g., "Some in U.S. Voting with Their Feet," by Rick Lyman, Monday, February 7, 2005, *New York Times*, or Andrew Buncombe, "Oh Canada, Here We Come: With U.S. Moving in a Different Direction, They're Moving North," Sunday, January 20, 2005, *Seattle Post-Intelligencer*.

[48] Calhoun (1988, p. 225).

media firms are now working together toward the creation of "electronic equivalents of gated communities."[49] Although the market segments they identify are not often explicitly based on political views, their "lifestyle" categories are hardly independent of political leanings. "Segment-making media," – those that "encourage small slices of society to talk to themselves" – are on the rise, while "society-making media" – "those that have the potential to get all those segments to talk to each other" – are on the downslide.[50] In addition to reducing the amount of direct exposure to dissonant views through media, specialized media and fragmented audiences may have secondary negative effects on interpersonal communication because the experience of shared viewing or reading is often what provides fuel for conversations across partisan lines.[51]

It would also advance the cause of hearing the other side if people had more weak ties in their social networks. This is the reason, for example, that those who work outside the home are more exposed to oppositional views than those who do not; work gives people more weak social relationships that are, nonetheless, ongoing relationships involving social interaction. By promoting weak ties, I do not intend yet another argument against automatic tellers and the like, for these fleeting encounters rarely stimulate much political dialogue. But, as Conover, Leonard, and Searing have suggested: "An adequate theory of democratic citizenship suitable to a pluralistic culture ought to be able to account for contexts in which it is appropriate to think of citizenship among 'friends' and also for contexts where it is appropriate to think of citizenship among 'strangers.'"[52]

If conversations are often uncomfortable, are there other ways to communicate political difference? Beyond political talk, we cannot help but make some political statements simply by the way we live our lives. For example, by being in the workplace, a woman makes a political statement whether she intends to or not.[53] Such nonverbal communication of political views is probably much less threatening and uncomfortable than verbal confrontation. But even these subtle "statements"

---

[49] Turow (1997, p. 2).
[50] Turow (1997).
[51] Katz (1996).
[52] Conover, Leonard, & Searing (1993, p. 169).
[53] Reardon (1995).

are not made without controversy, that is, without the need to defend one's behavior to others.

Political Talk, in Theory and in Practice

I began this book by noting that many different brands of democratic theory concurred on the importance of being exposed to non–like-minded political views. It matters little whether you come at this topic from the classic liberal tradition, from a communitarian emphasis, as a postmodernist, as a civic republican, or as any variant thereof. All agree that citizens are improved by cross-cutting exposure. That said, none of the existing theories appear to do a good job of taking into account the social psychological tensions of mixed political company. We are told that the "social" has reemerged as extremely important in the lexicon of political science,[54] and yet in our theories there has been surprisingly little acknowledgment of the social tensions of citizenship.[55]

From a theoretical perspective, the psychological tension is there precisely because most Americans adhere neither wholly to a liberal democratic tradition of individualism nor to the purely communitarian impulse toward group consensus. Most people want to get along with others; they would prefer consensus to political disagreement. But given diverse viewpoints, they maximize their chances of achieving "community" by gravitating toward like-minded others.

The remarkable popularity of nostalgic images of community leads one to wonder whether this concept has been oversold. In political and social commentary, there is a tremendous emphasis on (typically undocumented) loss of community and the need for more close-knit, trusting interpersonal relations. The same impulse that attracts people to the notion of more trusting face-to-face networks is what motivates the extreme popularity of gated communities and other homogeneous living environments. Close interpersonal networks among homogeneous people are better for creating trust and a strong sense of community identity, but they will not adequately serve the needs of a highly pluralistic political culture. The opportunity to live among people like

---

[54] Zuckerman (2004).

[55] Jane Mansbridge's (1980) studies of deliberation in real world organizations are an important exception to this tendency for theory and practice to ignore one another.

one's self is attractive precisely because community is much easier in a homogeneous environment.[56]

Given a forced choice between promoting like-minded networks and political activism, or heterogeneous networks and tolerance, in the contemporary political environment I would come down on the side of promoting greater heterogeneity. I can identify no intrinsic reason why participation should be valued more or less than tolerance. Nonetheless, I deem mixed company of greater importance for several reasons. For one, whereas neither deliberation nor participation may be a "natural" act, the tendency to gravitate toward like-minded others appears to be fairly universal. I have found no country in which people have a greater number of non–like-minded political discussants than like-minded ones.[57] Homogeneous networks occur regularly, probably because they offer their own, nonpolitical rewards. It is intrinsically reassuring and rewarding for people to see that others share their perspectives. For this reason, like-minded interactions are unlikely to need much encouragement. The need for solidarity and cooperation with others in day to day life will naturally produce plenty of relationships of this kind.

Homogeneous political networks can be a force for positive change *or* a source of intolerance and extremism. Heterogeneous political networks, on the other hand, convey many potential benefits, with lowered levels of participation the sole negative outcome. Short of unrealistic goals nearing 100 percent turnout, it is not clear whether higher turnout would substantially change political outcomes.[58] Given that people have a well-documented tendency to assume that others around them share their political views – even when this assumption is erroneous – the deck is further stacked against recognizing others' oppositional perspectives. Accuracy aside, the recognition of homogeneous

---

[56] Indeed, as Lasch (1995) notes, like-minded organizations such as advocacy groups often refer to themselves as "communities."

[57] Mutz (2001).

[58] Whether or not turnout would change electoral outcomes has been the subject of considerable research, though the answer appears to be complex and depends on class cleavages, what level of office one considers, and so forth. Martinez and Gill (2002), for example, suggest that even large changes in turnout would at most have only a very tiny effect on the presidential vote.

viewpoints comes easily, whereas heterogeneous views are often not recognized as such.

Future models connecting the quality and quantity of social interaction to democratic values need to take into account the functions served by both homogeneous and heterogeneous social interaction. But what theorists often portray as a choice between passive disengagement from one's fellow citizens or mindless conformity to a community consensus is not an either–or choice from the perspective of citizens. The norm is neither thumbing one's nose at one's neighbor nor being led sheeplike to endorse community opinion in order to get along with others. It is precisely because of the tension between these two impulses – the desire to get along peaceably with one's fellows and the desire to maintain one's independence of perspective – that political conversation is so tenuous. If conversation is going to be central to democratic life, as political philosophers such as John Dewey have advocated, then we need a realistic theory of conversation that addresses this tension.

Deliberative theorists have certainly thought about these questions,[59] but they have not gone so far as to suggest in concrete terms how people might interact with one another in mixed company, and yet simultaneously pursue active lives as political citizens. In this sense the political philosophy surrounding conversation is extremely removed from the everyday life of politics as experienced by most Americans.

Some suggest that disagreement is best relegated to contexts where formal rules of engagement already exist – that is, among elite legislatures or other formal bodies. I disagree. It is true that most informal conversations will fall well short of deliberative ideals. When real people argue about politics with friends and associates, they probably will not formulate new arguments or articulate reasons entirely by themselves as deliberative theory advocates. After all, even those pundits who argue as "professionals" are mostly rehashing preexisting political arguments. But citizens do need to be skilled at picking among these competing arguments, and at circulating them among themselves, trying them out in informal conversation and discarding those that do not

---

[59] Gutmann & Thompson (1996), for example, include "reciprocity" as one of the three prerequisites for deliberation, and this concept incorporates some characteristics necessary to ease tensions in interactions.

ring true. The marketplace of ideas will not work properly if political elites are the only ones involved.

The alternative would be to promote a set of norms for informal political discourse. The important skill of citizenship is not so much knowing everything there is to know about all conceivable political issues, so one can debate them knowledgeably. Instead, both informal deliberation and participation involve building and maintaining social and political networks, and both activities inevitably involve practical skills for social interaction. Networks facilitate political activism, as well as cross-cutting political discourse. Thus any theory of civic skills must take into account that citizens are embedded in networks of social, as well as political, relationships.

Manners for social interaction are taught from a very young age, and adults can even take whole courses on the finer points of such skills, but there is little if any instruction given to citizens in the practical skills of politics. By this I do not mean that ordinary citizens should be taught how to stuff fund-raising envelopes in the basement of the community center. Nor do I mean that they need to learn how to run political campaigns – though interestingly these skills *are* now taught as regular degree programs. Instead, we need instruction, and explicit norms, for how political differences should be handled respectfully in informal discourse. How can one be a successful advocate of political ideas without isolating one's self from those whose ideas differ? Only when such skills are equitably distributed – the ability to build and maintain diverse networks, and to evaluate and promote ideas through them – will the metaphor of a marketplace of political ideas ring true for American political culture.

As it now stands, the tension between the attributes of a social environment that would be best for participatory democracy and the kind that would be ideal for deliberative democracy is very real. As Schudson has suggested, when it comes to political involvement, "Sometimes it is necessary to take great risks, but in the long run, a desirable civic life is one where people can participate at acceptable levels of risk."[60] Americans will seldom risk life and limb to express their political views; however, those are not the only risks that count. Clearly not all citizens feel they can speak their minds freely without repercussions for

[60] Schudson (1998, p. 313).

their public or private lives. And yet the goal of reducing risks, both individual and collective, is an extremely valuable one that has yet to be incorporated into political theory or practical politics. Unfortunately, the repercussions of remaining silent in the face of controversy or of seeking out strictly like-minded others may be far greater. If the highly participatory segments of the population tend to expose themselves mainly to reinforcement, then they will not be very successful at promoting their political ideas nor at tolerating oppositional views.

References

Ackerman, B., & Fishkin, J. S. (2004). *Deliberation Day*. New Haven, CT: Yale University Press.

Allport, G. W. (1954). *The Nature of Prejudice*. Reading, MA: Addison-Wesley.

Almond, G. A. (1995, November 17). *The Civic Culture: Prehistory, Retrospect and Prospect* (Research Monograph Series). Irvine: University of California, Irvine, School of Social Sciences. Paper originally presented at the Center for the Study of Democracy and the Department of Politics and Society, University of California, Irvine.

Almond, G. A., & Verba, S. (Eds.). (1989a). *The Civic Culture Revisited*. Newbury Park, CA: Sage.

Almond, G. A., & Verba, S. (Eds.). (1989b). *The Civic Culture: Political Attitudes and Democracy in Five Nations*. Newbury Park, CA: Sage. (Original work published 1963).

Altemeyer, B. (1997). *The Authoritarian Specter*. Cambridge, MA: Harvard University Press.

Alvarez, R. M., & Brehm, J. (1995). American Ambivalence toward Abortion Policy. *American Journal of Political Science* 39 (November), 1055–1082.

Amir Y. (1976). The Role of Intergroup Contact in Change of Prejudice and Race Relations. In P. A. Katz (Eds.), *Towards the Elimination of Racism* (pp. 245–280). New York: Pergamon.

Arendt, H. (1968). *Between Past and Future: Eight Exercises in Political Thought*. New York: Viking Press.

Arrow, K. (1972). Gifts and Exchanges. *Philosophy and Public Affairs* 1 (Summer), 343–362.

Asch, S. (1952). *Social Psychology*. Englewood Cliffs, NJ: Prentice-Hall.

Baldassare, M. (1985). Trust in Local Government. *Social Science Quarterly* 66 (September), 704–712.

Barabas, J. (2004). How Deliberation Affects Policy Opinions. *American Political Science Review* 98 (4), 687–701.

Barber, B. (1984). *Strong Democracy: Participatory Politics for a New Age.* Berkeley: University of California Press.

Barker, D. C., & Hansen, S. (2005). All Things Considered: Systematic Cognitive Processing and Electoral Decision-Making. *Journal of Politics* 67 (2), 319–344.

Bartels, L. M. (2002). Beyond the Running Tally: Partisan Bias in Political Perceptions. *Political Behavior* 24 (2), 117–150.

Beck, P. A., Dalton, R. J., & Huckfeldt, R. R. (1995). Cross-National Election Studies: United States Study, 1992 (Version ICPSR) [Data file].

Bellah, R. N., Madsen, R., Sullivan, W. M., Swidler, A., & Tipton, S. M. (1985). *Habits of the Heart: Individualism and Commitment in American Life.* Berkeley: University of California Press.

Benhabib, S. (1992). *Situating the Self.* New York: Routledge.

Berelson, B., Lazarsfeld, P. F., & McPhee, W. N. (1954). *Voting: A Study of Opinion Formation in a Presidential Campaign.* Chicago: The University of Chicago Press.

Berinsky, A. J. (1999). The Two Faces of Public Opinion. *American Journal of Political Science* 43 (4), 1209–1230.

Berman, S. (1997). Civil Society and the Collapse of the Weimar Republic. *World Politics,* April, pp. 401–429.

Blakely, E. J., & Snyder, M. G. (1997). *Fortress America: Gated Communities in the United States.* Washington, DC: Brookings Institution Press.

Blau, P. M. (1977). *Inequality and Heterogeneity.* New York: The Free Press.

Blau, P. M. (1994). *Structural Contexts of Opportunities.* Chicago: University of Chicago Press.

Breckler, S. J. (1994). A Comparison of Numerical Indexes for Measuring Attitude Ambivalence. *Educational and Psychological Measurement* 54 (2), 350–365.

Brown, R., & Hewstone, M. (2005). An Integrative Theory of Intergroup Contact. *Advances in Experimental Social Psychology* 37, 255–343.

Brown, T. A. (1981). On Contextual Change and Partisan Attitudes. *British Journal of Political Science* 11, 427–448.

Burns, N., Kinder, D. R., & the National Election Studies. (2003). National Election Studies 2002: Pre-/Post-Election Study [Data set]. Ann Arbor: University of Michigan Center for Political Studies.

Burnstein, E., & Sentis, K. (1981). Attitude polarization in groups. In R. E. Petty, T. M. Ostrom, & T. C. Brock (Eds.), *Cognitive Responses in Persuasion.* Hillsdale, NJ: Lawrence Erlbaum.

Burnstein, E., Vinokur, A., & Trope, Y. (1973). Interpersonal Comparison versus Persuasive Argumentation: A More Direct Test of Alternative Explanations for Group-induced Shifts in Individual Choice. *Journal of Experimental Social Psychology* 9, 236–245.

Button, M., & Mattson, K. (1999). Deliberative Democracy in Practice: Challenges and Prospects for Civic Deliberation. *Polity 31* (4), 609–637.

Calhoun, C. (1988). Populist Politics, Communication Media and Large Scale Societal Integration. *Sociological Theory 6* (3), 219–241.

Campbell, A., Converse, P. E., Miller, W. E., & Stokes, D. E. (1960). *The American Voter*. New York: Wiley.

Campbell, D. E. (2002, April 25–28). *Getting Along versus Getting Ahead: Why the Absence of Partisan Competition Leads to High Voter Turnout*. Paper presented at the annual meeting of the Midwest Political Science Association, Chicago.

Campbell, J. E. (1997). *The Presidential Pulse of Congressional Elections*, 2nd ed. Lexington: The University Press of Kentucky.

Conover, P. J., Leonard, S. T., & Searing, D. D. (1993). Duty Is a Four-Letter Word: Democratic Citizenship in the Liberal Polity. In G. E. Marcus & R. L. Hanson (Eds.), *Reconsidering the Democratic Public* (pp. 147–172). University Park: Pennsylvania State University Press.

Conover, P. J., & Searing, D. D. (1998, April). *Political Discussion and the Politics of Identity*. Paper presented at the annual meeting of the Midwest Political Science Association, Chicago.

Converse, P. E. (1964). The Nature of Belief Systems in Mass Publics. In D. Apter (Ed.), *Ideology and Discontent* (pp. 206–261). New York: The Free Press.

Cook, S. W. (1984). Cooperative Interaction in Multiethnic Contexts. In N. Miller & M. B. Brewer (Eds.), *Groups in Contact: The Psychology of Desegregation* (pp. 155–185). Orlando, FL: Academic Press.

Cook, T. D., & Campbell, D. T. (1979). *Quasi-Experimentation: Design and Analysis Issues*. Boston: Houghton Mifflin.

Cotton, J. L. (1985). Cognitive Dissonance in Selective Exposure. In D. Z. a. J. Bryant (Ed.), *Selective Exposure to Communication* (pp. 11–33). Hillsdale, NJ: Erlbaum.

Cushing, R., & Bishop, B. (2004, December 3–4). *The Polarization of American Politics: Myth or Reality?* First panel at the Princeton University Conference sponsored by the Center for the Study of Democratic Politics and the Program in Leadership Studies of the Woodrow Wilson School of Public and International Affairs, Princeton, NJ.

Dalton, R. J., Beck, P. A., & Huckfeldt, R. (1998). Partisan Cues and the Media: Information Flows in the 1992 Presidential Election. *American Political Science Review 92* (1),111–126.

Dalton, R. J., Beck, P. A., Huckfeldt, R., & Koetzle, W. (1998). A Test of Media-Centered Agenda Setting: Newspaper Content and Public Interest in a Presidential Election. *Political Communication 15* (4), 463–481.

Davis, J. A. (1982). Achievement Variables and Class Cultures. *American Sociological Review 47* (5), 569–586.

Davis, M. H. (1983). Measuring Individual Differences in Empathy: Evidence for a Multidimensional Approach. *Journal of Personality and Social Psychology* 44 (January), 113–126.

Delli Carpini, M. X., & Keeter, S. (1996). *What Americans Know about Politics and Why It Matters*. New Haven, CT: Yale University Press.

Dewey, J. (1937). Democracy as a Way of Life. In R. R. Ammerman & M. G. Singer, (eds.), *Introductory Readings in Philosophy* (pp. 276–277). Dubuque, IA: Wm. C. Brown.

Eliasoph, N. (1998). *Avoiding Politics: How Americans Produce Apathy in Everyday Life*. Cambridge: Cambridge University Press.

Elshtain, J. B. (1995). *Democracy on Trial*. New York: Basic Books.

Farrar, C., Fishkin, J., Green, D., List, C., Luskin, R., & Paluck, E. (2003). *Experimenting with Deliberative Democracy: Effects on Policy Preferences and Social Choice*. Research paper, The Center for Deliberative Democracy, Stanford University, http://cdd.stanford.edu/research/papers/2003/experimenting.pdf.

Fearon, J. (1998). Deliberation as Discussion. In J. Elster (Ed.), *Deliberative Democracy* (pp. 44–68). Cambridge: Cambridge University Press.

Fiorina, M. P. (1999). Extreme Voices: A Dark Side of Civic Engagement. In T. Skocpol & M. P. Fiorina (Eds.), *Civic Engagement in American Democracy* (pp. 395–426). Washington, DC: Brookings Institution Press.

Fischer, C. S. (1999). Uncommon Values, Diversity and Conflict in City Life. In N. J. Smelser & J. C. Alexander (Eds.), *Diversity and Its Discontents* (pp. 213–227). Princeton, NJ: Princeton University Press.

Fishkin, J. S. (1991). *Democracy and Deliberation: New Directions for Democratic Reform*. New Haven, CT: Yale University Press.

Fishkin, J. S. (1996). *The Voice of the People: Public Opinion and Democracy*. New Haven, CT: Yale University Press.

Franklin, M. (2004). *Voter Turnout and the Dynamics of Electoral Competition in Established Democracies since 1945*. Cambridge: Cambridge University Press.

Freedman, J. L., & Sears, D. O. (1965). Selective Exposure. In L. Berkowitz (Ed.), *Advances in Social Psychology* (Vol. 2, pp. 57–97) New York: Academic Press.

Frey, W. H. (1995). The New Geography of Population Shifts: Trends toward Balkanization. In R. Farley (Ed.), *State of the Union: America in the 1990s* (Vol. 2). New York: Russell Sage.

Friedman, D., & McAdam, D. (1992). Identity Incentives and Activism: Networks, Choices and the Life of a Social Movement. In C. Mueller & A. Morris (Eds.), *Frontiers in Social Movement Theory* (pp. 156–173). New Haven, CT: Yale University Press.

Funk, C. L. (2001, April). *What's Not to Like? Explaining Public Disinterest in Politics*. Paper presented at the annual meeting of the Midwest Political Science Association, Chicago.

Gibson, J. L. (1999). *Social Networks, Civil Society, and the Prospects for Consolidating Russia's Democratic Transition* [Typescript]. St. Louis: Washington University, Department of Political Science.

Giles, M. W., & Dantico, M. K. (1982). Political Participation and Neighborhood Social Context Revisited. *American Journal of Political Science 26* (February), 144–150.

Gimpel, J. G., Dyck, J., & Shaw, D. R. (2004). Registrants, Voters and Turnout Variability across Neighborhoods. *Political Behavior 26* (4), 343–375.

Granovetter, M. (1973). The Strength of Weak Ties. *American Journal of Sociology 78* (May), 1360–1380.

Gray, J. (1995, January 22). Does Democracy Have a Future? *New York Times Book Review*.

Green, D., Palmquist, B., and Schickler, E. 2002. *Partisan Hearts and Minds: Political Parties and the Social Identities of Voters.* New Haven, CT: Yale University Press.

Green, M. C., Visser, P. S., & Tetlock, P. E. (2000). Coping with Accountability Cross-Pressures: Low-Effort Evasive Tactics and High-Effort Quests for Complex Compromises. *Personality and Social Psychology Bulletin 26,* 1380–1391.

Guge, M., & Meffert, M. F. (1998, April). *The Political Consequences of Attitudinal Ambivalence.* Paper presented at the annual meeting of the Midwest Political Science Association, Chicago.

Gutmann, A., & Thompson, D. (1996). *Democracy and Disagreement.* Cambridge, MA: Harvard Belknap Press.

Habermas, J. (1989). *The Structural Transformation of the Public Sphere.* Cambridge, MA: MIT Press.

Harrison, R. J., & Bennett, C. E. (1995). Racial and Ethnic Diversity. In R. Farley (Ed.), *State of the Union: America in the 1990s* (Vol. 2) New York: Russell Sage.

Hewstone, M., & Cairns, E. (2001). Social Psychology and Intergroup Conflict. In D. Chirot & M. E. P. Seligman (Eds.), *Ethno-Political Warfare: Causes, Consequences, and Possible Solutions* (pp. 319–342). Washington, DC: American Psychological Association.

Hibbing, J. R., & Theiss-Morse, E. (2002). *Stealth Democracy: Americans' Belief about How Government Should Work.* Cambridge: Cambridge University Press.

Hochschild, J. L. (1981). *What's Fair? American Beliefs about Distributive Justice.* Cambridge, MA: Harvard University Press.

Hochschild, J. L. (1993). Disjunction and Ambivalence in Citizens' Political Outlooks. In G. E. Marcus & R. L. Hanson (Eds.), *Reconsidering the Democratic Public* (pp. 187–210). University Park: Pennsylvania State University Press.

Horan, P. M. (1971). Social Positions and Political Cross-Pressures: A Re-Examination. *American Sociological Review 36* (August), 650–660.

Hovland, C. I., Janis, I. L., & Kelley, H. H. (1953). *Communication and Persuasion: Psychological Studies of Opinion Change*. New Haven, CT: Yale University Press.

Huckfeldt, R. R. (1979). Political Participation and the Neighborhood Social Context. *American Journal of Political Science* 23 (November), 579–592.

Huckfeldt, R. R. (1986). *Politics in Context: Assimilation and Conflict in Urban Neighborhoods*. New York: Agathon Press.

Huckfeldt, R. R., Johnson, P., & Sprague, J. (2004). *Political Disagreement: The Survival of Diverse Opinions within Communication Networks*. Cambridge: Cambridge University Press.

Huckfeldt, R. R., Mendez, J. M., & Osborn, T. (2004). Disagreement, Ambivalence, and Engagement: The Political Consequences of Heterogeneous Networks. *Political Psychology* 25 (1), 65–95.

Huckfeldt, R., & Sprague, J. (1995a). *Citizens, Politics, and Social Communication: Information and Influence in an Election Campaign*. Cambridge: Cambridge University Press.

Huckfeldt, R., & Sprague, J. (1995b). *Political Information and Communication among Citizens: Human Capital in an Election Campaign*. Proposal submitted to the National Science Foundation.

Hulbert, A. (2005). Unpersuasive: Why the SAT's New Essay Question Reinforces America's Allergy to Real Argument. *New York Times Magazine*, May 29, pp. 15–16.

Inglehart, R., Basanez, M., Diez-Medrano, J., Halman, L., & Luijkx, R. (Eds.). (2004). *Human Beliefs and Values*. Mexico City: Siglo XXI.

Jackson, E. F., & Curtis R. F. (2004, August). European and World Values Surveys Integrated Data File, 1999–2002 (Second ICPSR Version). Ann Arbor, MI: Inter-University Consortium for Political and Social Research.

Jackson, E. F., & Curtis, R. F. (1972). Effects of Vertical Mobility and Status Inconsistency: A Body of Negative Evidence. *American Sociological Review* 37 (6), 701–713.

Jalali, R., & Lipset, S. M. (1992, Winter). Racial and Ethnic Conflicts: A Global Perspective. *Political Science Quarterly* 107 (4), 585–606.

Karatnycky, A. (1999). The Decline of Illiberal Democracy. *Journal of Democracy* 10 (January), 112–125.

Katz, E. (1996). And Deliver Us from Segmentation. *Annals of the American Academy of Political and Social Science* 546, 22–33.

Kenny, C. B. (1992). Political Participation and Effects from the Social Environment. *American Journal of Political Science* 36 (February), 259–267.

Kingwell, M. (1995). *A Civil Tongue: Justice, Dialogue, and the Politics of Pluralism*. University Park: Pennsylvania State University Press.

Klinker, P. (2004). Red and Blue Scare: The Continuing Diversity of the American Electoral Landscape. *The Forum* 2 (2), Article 2.

Knight, J., & Johnson, J. (1994). Aggregation and Deliberation: On the Possibility of Democratic Legitimacy. *Political Theory* 22 (2), 277–296.

Knoke, D. (1990). *Political Networks: The Structuralist Perspective*. Cambridge: Cambridge University Press.

Kuklinski, J. H., Riggle, E., Ottati, V., Schwarz, N., & Wyer, R. S., Jr. (1991). The Cognitive and Affective Bases of Political Tolerance Judgments. *American Journal of Political Science 35* (February), 1–27.

Lasch, C. (1995). *The Revolt of the Elites and the Betrayal of Democracy*. New York: W. W. Norton.

Laumann, E. (1973). *Bonds of Pluralism: The Form and Substance of Urban Social Networks*. New York: Wiley Interscience.

Lavine, H. (2001). The Electoral Consequences of Ambivalence toward Presidential Candidates. *American Journal of Political Science 45* (4), 915–929.

Lazarsfeld, P. F., Berelson, B., & Gaudet, H. (1944). *The People's Choice*. New York: Duell, Sloan and Pearce.

Leighley, J. E. (1990). Social Interaction and Contextual Influences on Political Participation. *American Politics Quarterly 18* (October), 459–475.

Leonard, M. (2004). Bonding and Bridging Social Capital: Reflections from Belfast. *Sociology 38* (5), 927–944.

Lessl, T. M. (1998, November). *The Darwin Fish Survey: A Critical Analysis*. Paper presented at the meeting of the National Communication Association, New York.

Levy, F. (1995). Incomes and Income Inequality. In R. Farley (Ed.), *State of the Union: America in the 1990s*, Vol. 1: *Economic Trends* (pp. 1–57). New York: Russell Sage.

Macedo, S. (Ed.). (1999). *Deliberative Politics: Essays on Democracy and Disagreement*. Oxford: Oxford University Press.

MacKinnon, C. A. (1989). *Toward a Feminist Theory of the State*. Cambridge, MA: Harvard University Press.

Manin, B. (1987). On Legitimacy and Political Deliberation. *Political Theory 15* (3), 338–368.

Mansbridge, J. (1980). *Beyond Adversary Democracy*. New York: Basic Books.

Mansbridge, J. (1986). *Why We Lost the ERA*. Chicago: University of Chicago Press.

Mansbridge, J. (1999). Everyday Talk in the Deliberative System. In S. Macedo (Ed.), *Deliberative Politics: Essays on Democracy and Disagreement* (pp. 211–239). Oxford: Oxford University Press.

Marcus, G. E. (2002). *The Sentimental Citizen: Emotion in Democratic Politics*. University Park: Pennsylvania State University Press.

Marcus, G. E., Sullivan, J. L., Theiss-Morse, E., & Wood, S. L. (1995). *With Malice toward Some: How People Make Civil Liberties Judgments*. Cambridge: Cambridge University Press.

Martin, J. (2004, February 4). Miss Manners: Polite vs. Political Conversation. *Washington Post*.

Martinez, M. D., & Gill, J. (2002, September). *Have Turnout Effects Really Declined? Testing and Partisan Implications of Marginal Voters*. Paper presented at the annual meeting of the American Political Science Association, Boston.

Massey, D., & Denton, N. (1993). *American Apartheid*. Cambridge, MA: Harvard University Press.

McAdam, D. (1986). Recruitment to High Risk Activism: The Case of Freedom Summer. *American Journal of Sociology 92*, 64–90.

McPhee, W. N., Smith, R. B., & Ferguson, J. (1963). A Theory of Informal Social Influence. In W. N. McPhee (Ed.), *Formal Theories of Mass Behavior* (pp. 74–103). New York: The Free Press.

McPherson, J. M., Popielarz, P. A., & Drobnic, S. (1992). Social Networks and Organizational Dynamics. *American Sociological Review 57* (April), 153–170.

McPherson, J. M., & Rotolo, T. (1996). Testing a Dynamic Model of Social Composition: Diversity and Change in Voluntary Groups. *American Sociological Review 61* (April), 179–202.

McPherson, J. M., & Smith-Lovin, L. (1986). Sex Segregation in Voluntary Associations. *American Sociological Review 51*, 61–79.

McPherson, J. M., & Smith-Lovin, L. (1987). Homophily in Voluntary Organizations: Status Distance and the Composition of Face-to-Face Groups. *American Sociological Review 52*, 370–379.

Mead, G. H. (1934). *Mind, Self and Society*. Chicago: University of Chicago Press.

Mendelberg, T. (2002). The Deliberative Citizen: Theory and Evidence. In M. X. Delli Carpini, L. Huddy, & R. Y. Shapiro (Eds.), *Political Decision Making, Deliberation and Participation: Research in Micropolitics* (Vol. 6, pp. 151–193). Greenwich, CT: JAI Press.

Merton, R. K. (1968). *Social Theory and Social Structure*, enlarged ed. New York: The Free Press.

Mill, J. S. (1956). *On Liberty*. Indianapolis: Bobbs-Merrill. (Original work published 1859).

Mill, J. S. (1969). Bentham. In *Collected Works: Essays on Ethics, Religion, and Society* (Vol. 10): Toronto: Routledge & Kegan Paul.

Morrell, M. E. (2000, April). *Participatory Democracy, Deliberative Structures, and Empathy*. Paper presented at the annual meeting of the Midwest Political Science Association, Chicago.

Muhlberger, P., & Butts, C. (1998, April). *An Experiment in Deliberative Democracy: Politics Shaping Citizens*. Paper presented at the annual meeting of the Midwest Political Science Association, Chicago.

Muirhead, R. (2003, September). *In Defense of Partisanship*. Paper presented at the annual meeting of the American Political Science Association, Philadelphia.

Muirhead, R. (2005, January 24). *Left and Right: A Defense of Party Spirit*. Paper presented at the University of Texas, Austin.

Mutz, D. C. (1998). *Impersonal Influence*. Cambridge: Cambridge University Press.

Mutz, D. C. (2001, September). *Where in the World Is in the Public Sphere? A 12 Country Comparison of Mass and Interpersonal Communication*. Paper presented at the annual meeting of the American Political Science Association, San Francisco.

Mutz, D. C. (2002a). The Consequences of Cross-Cutting Networks for Political Participation. *American Journal of Political Science 46* (4), 838–855.

Mutz, D. C. (2002b). Cross-Cutting Social Networks: Testing Democratic Theory in Practice. *American Political Science Review 96* (March), 111–126.

Mutz, D. C., & Martin, P. S. (2001). Facilitating Communication across Lines of Political Difference: The Role of Mass Media. *American Political Science Review 95* (1), 97–114.

Mutz, D. C., & Mondak, J. J. (1997, April). *What's So Great about League Bowling?* Paper presented at the annual meeting of the Midwest Political Science Association, Chicago.

Mutz, D. C., & Mondak, J. J. (1998, April). *Democracy at Work: Contributions of the Workplace toward a Public Sphere*. Paper presented at the annual meeting of the Midwest Political Science Association, Chicago.

Mutz, D. C., & Mondak, J. J. (2002, September). *When Good Things Happen Because of Annoying Co-Workers: The Role of the Workplace in Fostering Political Tolerance*. Paper presented at the annual meeting of the American Political Science Association, Boston.

Mutz, D. C., & Mondak, J. J. (2006). The Workplace as a Context for Cross-Cutting Political Discourse. *Journal of Politics 68* (1).

Noelle-Neumann, E. (1984). *The Spiral of Silence: Public Opinion – Our Social Skin*. Chicago: University of Chicago Press.

Nunn, C. Z., Crockett, H. J., & Williams, J. A. (1978). *Tolerance for Nonconformity*. San Francisco: Jossey-Bass.

Oliver, J. E. (1999). The Effects of Metropolitan Economic Segregation on Local Civic Participation. *American Journal of Political Science 43* (1), 186–212.

Oliver, J. E. (2001). *Democracy in Suburbia*. Princeton, NJ: Princeton University Press.

Palmer, P. (1981). *The Company of Strangers*. New York: Crossroad/Herder & Herder.

Parietti, J. (1997). *The Book of Truly Stupid Business Quotes*. New York: Collins.

Park, R. E. (1967). The City: Suggestion for the Investigation of Human Behavior in the Urban Environment. In R. E. Park & E. W. Burgess (Eds.), *The City* (pp. 1–46). Chicago: University of Chicago Press. (Original work published 1916).

Pateman, C. (1970). *Participation and Democratic Theory*. Cambridge: Cambridge University Press.

Peng, K. P., & Nisbett, R. E. (1999). Culture, Dialectics and Reasoning about Contradiction. *American Psychologist 54*, 741–754.

Pettigrew, T. F. (1997). Generalized Intergroup Contact Effects on Prejudice. *Personality and Social Psychology Bulletin* 23 (February), 173–185.

Pettigrew, T. F. (1998). Intergroup Contact Theory. *Annual Review of Psychology 49*, 65–85.

Pettigrew, T. F., & Tropp, L. R. (2000). Does Intergroup Contact Reduce Prejudice? Recent Meta-Analytic Findings. In S. Oskamp (Ed.), *Reducing Prejudice and Discrimination: The Claremont Symposium on Applied Social Psychology* (pp. 93–114). Mahwah, NJ: Erlbaum.

Petty, R., & Cacioppo, J. T. (1979). Issue Involvement Can Increase or Decrease Persuasion by Enhancing Message-Relevant Cognitive Responses. *Journal of Personality and Social Psychology 37*, 915–926.

Piaget, J. (1932). *The Moral Judgment of the Child* (M. Gabain, Trans.). New York: Harcourt, Brace.

Pool, I. d. S., Abelson, R. P., & Popkin, S. (1965). *Candidates, Issues and Strategies: A Computer Simulation of the 1960 and 1964 Elections.* Cambridge, MA: MIT Press.

Popielarz, P., & McPherson, J. M. (1995). On the Edge or in Between: Niche Position, Niche Overlap, and the Duration of Voluntary Association Memberships. *American Journal of Sociology 101*, 698–720.

Price, V., & Cappella, J. N. (2001, May). *Online Deliberation and Its Influence: The Electronic Dialogue Project in Campaign 2000.* Paper presented at the annual meeting of the American Association for Public Opinion Research, Montreal.

Priester, J. R., & Petty, R. E. (2001). Extending the Bases of Subjective Attitudinal Ambivalence: Interpersonal and Intrapersonal Antecedents of Evaluative Tension. *Journal of Personality and Social Psychology 80* (1), 19–34.

Putnam, R. D. (1966). Political Attitudes and the Local Community. *American Political Science Review 60* (3), 640–654.

Putnam, R. D. (1996). Creating Reflective Dialogue. In S. Toulmin & B. Gustavsen (Eds.), *Beyond Theory: Changing Organizations through Participation* (pp. 41–52). Amsterdam: John Benjamins.

Reardon, K. (1995). *They Don't Get It, Do They?* New York: Little, Brown.

Reich, C., & Purbhoo, M. (1975). The Effects of Cross-Cultural Contact. *Canadian Journal of Behavioural Science 7* (October), 313–327.

Rosenberg, M. (1954–1955). Some Determinants of Political Apathy. *Public Opinion Quarterly 18* (Winter), 349–366.

Rosenstone, S., & Hansen, J. M. (1993). *Mobilization, Participation, and Democracy in America.* New York: Macmillan.

Sanders, L. M. (1997). Against Deliberation. *Political Theory 25* (3), 347–376.

Schauer, F. (1999). Talking as a Decision Procedure. In S. Macedo (Ed.), *Deliberative Politics: Essays on Democracy and Disagreement* (pp. 17–27). Oxford: Oxford University Press.

Schudson, M. (1992). Was There Ever a Public Sphere? If So, When? Reflections on the American Case. In C. Calhoun (Ed.), *Habermas and the Public Sphere* (pp. 143–163). Cambridge, MA: MIT Press.

Schudson, M. (1995). *The Power of News*. Cambridge, MA: Harvard University Press.

Schudson, M. (1997). Why Conversation Is Not the Soul of Democracy. *Critical Studies in Mass Communication 14* (4), 297–309.

Schudson, M. (1998). *The Good Citizen*. New York: The Free Press.

Scorza, J. A. (1998, September). *Uncivil Friendship: Emersonian Lessons for Democratic Disagreement*. Paper presented at the annual meeting of the American Political Science Association, Boston.

Sigelman, L., Bledsoe, T., Welch, S., & Combs, M. (1996). Making Contact? Black–White Social Interaction in an Urban Setting. *American Journal of Sociology 101* (March 5), 1306–1332.

Simmel, G. (1955). *Conflict and the Web of Group Affiliations* (K. H. Wolff, Trans.). New York: The Free Press.

Simon, A. F., & Sulkin, T. (2000, April). *Assessing Deliberation in Small Groups*. Paper presented at the annual meeting of the Midwest Political Science Association, Chicago.

Sniderman, P. M. (1981). *A Question of Loyalty*. Berkeley: University of California Press.

Steiner, I. D. (1966). Personality and the Resolution of Interpersonal Disagreements. In B. A. Maher (Ed.), *Progress in Experimental Personality Research* (pp. 195–239). New York: Academic Press.

Stolle, D., & Rochon, R. (1998). Are All Associations Alike? Member Diversity, Associational Type and the Creation of Social Capital. *American Behavioral Scientist 42* (1), 47–65.

Stouffer, S. (1955). *Communism, Conformity, and Civil Liberties*. New York: Doubleday.

Sullivan, J. L., Piereson, J., & Marcus, G. E. (1982). *Political Tolerance and American Democracy*. Chicago: University of Chicago Press.

Sunstein, C. (2000). Deliberative Trouble? Why Groups Go to Extremes. *Yale Law Journal 110* (October), 71–119.

Sunstein, C. (2002). The Law of Group Polarization. *Journal of Political Philosophy 10* (2), 175–195.

Tarrow, S. (1998). *Power in Movement: Social Movements and Contentious Politics*, 2nd ed. Cambridge: Cambridge University Press.

Theiss-Morse, E., Marcus, G. E., & Sullivan, J. L. (1993). Passion and Reason in Political Life: The Organization of Affect and Cognition and Political Tolerance. In G. E. Marcus & R. L. Hanson (Eds.), *Reconsidering the Democratic Public* (pp. 249–272). University Park: Pennsylvania State University Press.

Thompson, M. M., Zanna, M. P., & Griffin, D. W. (1995). Let's Not Be Indifferent about (Attitudinal) Ambivalence. In R. E. Petty & J. A. Krosnick (Eds.),

Attitude Strength: Antecedents and Consequences (pp. 361–386). Hillsdale, NJ: Erlbaum.

Turow, J. (1997). *Breaking Up America*. Chicago: University of Chicago Press.

Ulbig, S. G., & Funk, C. L. (1999). Conflict Avoidance and Political Participation. *Political Behavior 21* (3), 265–282.

Verba, S., & Nie, N. H. (1972). *Participation in America: Political Democracy and Social Equality*. Chicago: University of Chicago Press.

Verba, S., Schlozman, K. L., & Brady, H. E. (1995). *Voice and Equality: Civic Voluntarism in American Politics*. Cambridge, MA: Harvard University Press.

Warren, M. E. (1996). What Should We Expect from More Democracy? Radically Democratic Responses to Politics. *Political Theory 24* (2), 241–270.

Wattenberg, M. P. (1994). *The Decline of American Political Parties, 1952–1994*. Cambridge, MA: Harvard University Press.

Weber, L. M. (1998, April). *The Effect of Democratic Deliberation on Political Tolerance*. Paper presented at the annual meeting of the Midwest Political Science Association, Chicago.

Weigert, K. M. (1976). Intergroup Contact and Attitudes about a Third Group: A Survey of Black Soldiers' Perceptions. *International Journal of Group Tensions 6*, 110–124.

Wright, S. C., Aron, A., McLaughlin-Volpe, T., & Ropp, S. A. (1997). The Extended Contact Effect: Knowledge of Cross-Group Friendship and Prejudice. *Journal of Personality and Social Psychology 73* (1), 73–90.

Wuthnow, R. (1998). *Loose Connections: Joining Together in America's Fragmented Communities*. Cambridge, MA: Harvard University Press.

Wuthnow, R. (1999). The Culture of Discontent: Democratic Liberalism and the Challenge of Diversity in Late Twentieth Century America. In N. J. Smelser & J. C. Alexander (Eds.), *Diversity and Its Discontents* (pp. 19–36). Princeton, NJ: Princeton University Press.

Wyatt, R. O., Katz, E., Levinsohn, H., & Al-Haj, M. (1996). The Dimensions of Expression Inhibition: Perceptions of Obstacles to Free Speech in Three Cultures. *International Journal for Public Opinion Research 8*, 229–247.

Wyatt, R. O., & Liebes, T. (1995, March). *Inhibition: Factors That Inhibit Talk in Public and Private Spaces in Three Cultures*. Paper presented at the Annenberg School for Communication, Conference on Public Space, University of Pennsylvania, Philadelphia.

Yoon, C. K. (2003, February 11). Fish Evolve and Multiply, but Not in the Traditional Way. *New York Times*, Section F.

Young, I. M. (1996). Communication and the Other: Beyond Deliberative Democracy. In S. Benhabib (Ed.), *Democracy and Difference* (pp. 120–136). Princeton, NJ: Princeton University Press.

Zaller, J. (1992). *The Nature and Origins of Mass Opinion.* Cambridge: Cambridge University Press.

Zaller, J., & Feldman, S. (1992). A Simple Theory of the Survey Response: Answering Questions versus Revealing Preferences. *American Journal of Political Science* 36 (August), 579–616.

Zuckerman, A. S. (2004). *The Social Logic of Politics: Personal Networks as Contexts for Political Behavior.* Philadelphia: Temple University Press.

Index

Made in the USA
Columbia, SC
29 August 2018